WHY PHYSICIAN
HOME LOANS
FAIL

WHY PHYSICIAN
HOME LOANS
FAIL

how to **AVOID THE LAND MINES** *for a*

FLAWLESS HOME PURCHASE

JOSH METTLE

Advantage®

Copyright © 2014 by Josh Mettle

All rights reserved. No part of this book may be used or reproduced in any manner whatsoever without prior written consent of the author, except as provided by the United States of America copyright law.

Published by Advantage, Charleston, South Carolina.
Member of Advantage Media Group.

ADVANTAGE is a registered trademark and the Advantage colophon is a trademark of Advantage Media Group, Inc.

Printed in the United States of America.

ISBN: 978-1-59932-446-3
LCCN: 2014935720

This publication is designed to provide accurate and authoritative information in regard to the subject matter covered. It is sold with the understanding that the publisher is not engaged in rendering legal, accounting, or other professional services. If legal advice or other expert assistance is required, the services of a competent professional person should be sought.

Advantage Media Group is proud to be a part of the Tree Neutral® program. Tree Neutral offsets the number of trees consumed in the production and printing of this book by taking proactive steps such as planting trees in direct proportion to the number of trees used to print books. To learn more about Tree Neutral, please visit **www.treeneutral.com**. To learn more about Advantage's commitment to being a responsible steward of the environment, please visit **www.advantagefamily.com/green**

Advantage Media Group is a publisher of business, self-improvement, and professional development books and online learning. We help entrepreneurs, business leaders, and professionals share their Stories, Passion, and Knowledge to help others Learn & Grow. Do you have a manuscript or book idea that you would like us to consider for publishing? Please visit **advantagefamily.com** or call **1.866.775.1696**.

—— *A NOTE FROM THE AUTHOR* ——

If there is one thing my physician clients have taught me, it's that physicians are extraordinarily busy. You are likely to prefer the Cliff Notes version of whatever you read. I've written this book in anticipation that you will only read what is relevant to you and where you are in the home-buying process.

As such, the most important lessons are repeated in different areas of the book, using different real client examples. If you read this book cover to cover, you will notice some repetition. It is designed to ensure you do not miss the crucial lessons contained within.

Even as we wrote the book and went through the editing process, guidelines and rules were changing, forcing us to update as we were preparing to release. Understand that the mortgage business is fluid and constantly moving. What we've written is as accurate a depiction of the conventional, FHA, and physician mortgage landscape as humanly possible, knowing that underwriting guidelines and loan programs are in a constant state of flux. There are bound to be some parts of the book that are not 100 percent accurate for 100 percent of the mortgage loan programs available to physicians from coast to coast. However, we will continually update the online versions of the book to keep the text as accurate as possible as time goes on and guidelines unceasingly change.

Enjoy!

FOREWORD

BY JAMES M. DAHLE MD, FACEP, *AKA: The White Coat Investor*
Author of *The White Coat Investor: A Doctor's Guide to Personal Finance and Investing*

Physicians have more in common with successful artists, professional athletes, and even lottery winners than they might think. Due to unique talents and skills (and perhaps even a bit of luck), they command a high income despite having little financial knowledge or experience in navigating the business world. A successful business owner, on the other hand, acquired his high income and high net worth by developing to a high degree essential business, sales, marketing, accounting, investing, and even personal finance skills. When doctors step into the business world, exchanging scrubs for a business suit, they are at a marked disadvantage. Physicians are not taught, have never learned, and have never realized they need to possess knowledge that is commonplace for other people with similar incomes. If a doctor wants to be successful at business, investing, or personal finance, he will need to acquire this knowledge on his own. The book you hold in your hands will aid you by giving you a piece of this knowledge and the confidence that you can interact successfully with others in the business world.

Home ownership is considered by many to be a rite of passage or even the fulfillment of the American Dream. More importantly, home ownership is usually an important step on the pathway to significant wealth. Homeowners build wealth in several ways in which those who rent their humble abode do not. They receive significant tax breaks by deducting their mortgage loan interest and property taxes from their income. Homeowners benefit from financial appreciation of their home, and particularly, the land on which the home sits. They also increase their net worth each year, as the mortgage loan is paid down. Rent payments do not build wealth, but every payment made on an amortizing mortgage surely does. Perhaps the greatest benefit homeowners receive is when the mortgage is finally paid off. While they will still have significant housing expenses, such as property taxes, maintenance, repairs, and upgrades, they now live free of both rent and mortgage payments. For most physicians, a paid-off mortgage increases disposable income by thousands of dollars per month.

Home ownership is not for everyone, of course. There are many times in your life when you may end up financially better off renting a home than buying one. Residency, in particular, is a time when serious consideration of the benefits of renting your home should occur. However, the vast majority of physicians in stable, long-term positions should own their own home. A home is both an investment and a consumption item, and so it is important to not overextend yourself when selecting one. I generally recommend that physicians do not carry a mortgage larger than two times their gross income, and keep their housing expenses (mortgage payments, property taxes, insurance, utilities, repairs, and maintenance) to less than 20 percent of their gross income. Some exceptions occasionally have to be made, but they should be limited in both frequency and scope.

Once a physician has decided to purchase a home and determined how much he wants to pay for it, he has yet another decision to make: how to find and finance the home. You will find this book invaluable when making this decision. Physicians in their first five to ten years out of medical school often have a serious cash flow problem. Despite their high income, they face a large, high-interest student loan burden, a dramatically increased tax bill, and the need to save for both retirement and college. It often makes good financial sense to use extra cash to pay down student loans and contribute to retirement accounts rather than save up for a traditional house down payment. While a frugal physician can do all three of these things, many doctors choose to take advantage of physician-specific mortgage programs that allow them to avoid a large down payment, private mortgage insurance (PMI), and onerous income documentation requirements. While the interest rate, fees, risk of going "underwater" on the loan, total loan size, and monthly payment are all higher using a physician mortgage instead of a conventional loan with a 20 percent down payment, it can still make sense for many physician families to use these mortgages. Of course, these families should direct the money that would have been used for a down payment toward building wealth by paying down student loans and contributing to tax-advantaged retirement accounts, rather than simply increasing their standard of living.

I have purchased a mortgage, either on a new purchase or on a refinance, eight times in my life. Each time, I have learned something new about the mortgage lending and real estate business. The smoothest loan I have ever closed on was done through Josh Mettle, the author of this book. He is dedicated to helping physicians reach their financial goals, and acquiring the knowledge in this book will help you to do so. Armed with this knowledge, you will avoid the errors that numerous physicians, including me, have made in choosing mortgages, mortgage lenders, and Realtors.

If you enjoy learning about financial topics such as those discussed in this book, consider purchasing my recently published book, *The White Coat Investor: A Doctor's Guide to Personal Finance and Investing*. You are also invited to stop by The White Coat Investor website (http://whitecoatinvestor.com), where you will find a community of financially savvy doctors helping each other to get a "fair shake" on Wall Street. Enjoy your new home and good luck with your career and your finances!

TABLE OF CONTENTS

07 | A NOTE FROM THE AUTHOR

09 | FOREWORD

by James M. Dahle, MD/AKA: The White Coat Investor

19 | INTRODUCTION

    19 – Genesis of a Mortgage Debacle

    21 – Huge Conflict in Mortgage Lending

    23 – Why Write a Book About Mortgage Loans for Physicians?

    24 – What Are the Danger Zones?

    26 – About the Author

27 | CHAPTER 1: THE RENT-VERSUS-BUY CONUNDRUM

    29 – Problems and Challenges Physicians Face When Buying a Home

    31 – Common Challenges

    33 – What Criteria Should I Use to Choose a Mortgage Lender?

    34 – How to Navigate Through the Many Mortgage Products Out There

37 | CHAPTER 2: WHERE DO I START? FIND A REALTOR OR A LOAN OFFICER?

    38 – Why Preapproval Is Not Enough!

    40 – Six Things to Do When Searching for a Mortgage Lender

    44 – How to Find an Awesome Realtor

    46 – How to Buy a New Home a Long Way From Home

49 | CHAPTER 3: THE PHYSICIAN HOME LOAN

    49 – How Can I Find a Physician Home Loan Lender in My City?

    50 – What Is the Difference Between a Physician Home Loan and a Conventional Loan?

    53 – Physician Home Loan FAQs

67 | CHAPTER 4: HOME LOAN OPTIONS FOR THE GRADUATING MED STUDENT GOING INTO RESIDENCY

67 — *Why Resident Physicians Struggle the Most*

68 — *Typical Challenges Resident Physicians Face*

69 — *FHA or VA Home Loan*

70 — *Conventional Home Loan*

71 — *Physician Home Loan*

72 — *How Do I Know Which Loan Is Truly the Best Option?*

73 — *A True Story: Dr. Schwartz's Near-Disaster*

75 — *Lessons Learned*

77 | CHAPTER 5: HOME LOAN OPTIONS FOR THE RESIDENT OR FELLOW GOING INTO PRACTICE

77 — *Typical Challenges New Attending Physicians Face*

78 — *FHA, VA, or Down Payment*

79 — *Conventional Home Loan*

81 — *Physician Home Loan*

82 — *A True Story: Dr. Gilbertson*

83 — *Lessons Learned*

85 | CHAPTER 6: HOME LOAN OPTIONS FOR SELF-EMPLOYED AND 1099 CONTRACTOR PHYSICIANS

85 — *How Underwriting Views Self-Employed and 1099 Contractor Borrowers*

86 — *Income Verification for 1099 Contractor Physicians*

88 — *Income Verification for Self-Employed Physicians*

89 — *Conventional, FHA, VA*

90 — *Physician Home Loan*

91 — *A True Story: Dr. Finkel*

94 — *Lessons Learned*

97 | CHAPTER 7: WHAT TO EXPECT AT THE CLOSING

97 — *How to Prepare for the Closing*

98 — *Important Communication Between Your Lender and You*

99 — *Settlement Statement Review*

99 — *Your Cash to Close*

100 — *Timing of the Closing*

100 — *Signs of Trouble: When to Ask Questions*

101 — *Closing Remotely Before You Arrive at Your New Home*

103 — *FAQs About Your Home Loan Closing*

105 | CHAPTER 8: COMMON MISTAKES WHEN BUYING A HOME

105 — *Failing to Insist on a Full Credit and Income Approval*

106 — *Deciding on a Lender Purely Based on Cost*

108 — *Missing Purchase Contract Deadlines*

109 — *A True Story: Dr. Fish*

111 — *Lessons Learned*

115 | CHAPTER 9: KEY POINTS FOR PHYSICIANS

115 — *Overview of the Life of a Loan*

117 — *A True Story: Dr. Peters's Perfect Transaction*

119 — *Lesson Learned*

119 — *Six Steps to a Flawless Home Purchase*

1. *Choose a Mortgage Professional Who Can Educate and Truly Guide You*

2. *Verify Your Lender's Reputation*

3. *Obtain a Credit and Income Approval*

4. *Carefully Select Your Realtor*

5. *Stay in Communication*

6. *Be Proactive*

125 | APPENDIX A

131 | APPENDIX B

—————— *INTRODUCTION* ——————

In the post-mortgage-meltdown world of mortgage lending, physicians face more challenges and have a higher rate of underwriter decline than any other professionals I've worked with. It's shocking but true. Spend a few moments online in physician chat rooms where the topic is mortgage and you will read nightmare after nightmare story. It is truly scary.

GENESIS OF A MORTGAGE DEBACLE

Here is a real-life scenario based on a post I read in a physician chat room:

> A newly attending physician and his young wife are in the process of buying a new home and relocating across the county. Excited about the adventure and future ahead of them, they pack their belongings in the largest U-Haul trailer they could rent and drive to their new home state. The day before their closing deadline, they arrive and find their loan is not cleared to close. The bank wants to do an internal audit that will cause further delay. They are forced to wait for days without getting any clear response or timeline from the big national bank they were working with. They try everything, calling the loan officer, the processor. They drive to a local office and ask for a manager, all to no avail. The days turn into a full week of missed work, living in a hotel, and still no communica-

tion as to what is going on or if the loan will eventually be approved or declined.

Their week off, the big move week, is spent frantically trying to keep the real estate transaction together and pleading for updates from the loan officer as to when they might close. Unfortunately, the young physician's wife is due back at the law firm she works for and she's forced to leave, U-Haul van full of furniture and home still in limbo. The young couple cannot understand or get a straight answer as to why the bank is having difficulty processing and closing their loan.

Needless to say, they are extremely angry, which they have made very clear to the "pencil pushers" (the physician's exact words) processing their loan. The physician ends his post with, "And we wonder why there is/was a mortgage crisis."

This nightmare scenario is not unique. Unfortunately, we regularly receive calls from clients with similar stories, the cause of which is, typically, one or both of the following common mistakes made early in the loan process:

1. **The loan officer they are dealing with has no experience with physicians.** Most loan officers do not understand complicated physician employment contracts, closing on future income (before employment even begins), 1099 independent contractor positions, self-employed physician practices, student loans with IBR (income-based repayment), deferments, forbearances, or the complexity these factors bring to the underwriting process, and the effect they have on the final underwriting approval or

decline. Virtually all physicians deal with these issues at some point in their career; the average loan officer sees these issues only once in a blue moon and, consequently, misunderstands and mismanages them frequently.

2. **The physician client did not do sufficient research early enough in the process.** This is hard for clients to accept, but the reality is that many of the physicians we advise have a *very* complex loan to underwrite. There are often multiple moving pieces: new positions, complicated employment contracts, independent contractor employment, relocation across the country, student loans coming out of or into deferment, and limited down payments, which are often gifted or coming from relocation or sign-on bonuses. All of which can be a reason for decline by an underwriter using conventional underwriting guidelines.

Understand that from your logical perspective, you are the most intelligent, high-income, high-credit, dependable person you know. To the average loan officer and mortgage underwriter, your situation is confusing and doesn't fit the guidelines. Simply put, many physicians don't fit cleanly into the conventional underwriting "box."

HUGE CONFLICT IN MORTGAGE LENDING

There is a huge conflict in mortgage lending, which leads to most if not all of the ugly, last-minute, declined-loan situations such as the one described above.

Here's the truth: loan officers are paid to say yes. We only receive a commission if we can close your loan, so it behooves us to say, "Yes, I can get your loan done." Regrettably, some loan officers get too comfortable with this response, resulting in perilous consequences for unknowing homebuyers. It's not that most loan officers are bad or are lying. Unfortunately, they just don't know better. Most are not experienced enough with the complexities that are commonplace with physicians.

Conversely, mortgage underwriters are paid to say no. They are the gatekeepers and their job is to ensure that your loan meets the underwriting guidelines to the letter. If they say yes and approve your loan without your exactly fitting the underwriting guideline "box," the underwriter could be disciplined or even terminated. So, it has little to do with common sense or even your ability to service the debt and make on-time payments. It has everything to do with whether your loan fits the written underwriting guidelines the underwriters are given.

Most mortgage loans are bundled with other mortgage loans, securitized, and sold to entities such as Fannie Mae and Freddie Mac. As such, the underwriter has to certify that your loan meets those rigid guidelines. If the loan is approved and it doesn't meet those guidelines, the underwriter is accountable to the company that might have to buy the loan back, suffer any losses, and sit on the loan or sell it at a discount for a potentially huge loss. That's the world underwriters live in today. They are making decisions with hundreds of thousands of dollars, which equates to a lot of liability for them. They can tarnish their reputation or be fired for missing something or making mistakes. Most live in a world of fear and lose sleep about approving the wrong loan.

Because of this conflict between loan officers (yes) and underwriters (no), many physicians face problems during the underwriting process. This is why you, as a physician, should be better educated and prepared for the mortgage and home-buying process than anyone else.

The goal of this book is to help you:

- identify the potential pitfalls and avoid catastrophe when buying a home;
- prepare you for the mortgage and home buying process;
- find and select an expert loan officer and Realtor.

For a nationwide directory of professional loan officers specializing in physician home loans, visit www.usphysicianhomeloans.com.

WHY WRITE A BOOK ABOUT MORTGAGE LOANS FOR PHYSICIANS?

A few years back, I received a call from a panicked client who had Googled "physician home loans Utah" and had found one of my articles. He was a young man who had just finished medical school and was relocating to Utah for his residency at the University of Utah hospital. He was calling me from the road with his family out of earshot and having lunch as they made their way across country. He told me his story: He'd just received a call (while driving) from the loan officer who had preapproved him for his mortgage about a month earlier. The loan officer was "very sorry" to let him know the bank's underwriter had declined his loan. It turned out the loan officer who had preapproved him had not calculated his deferred student loans into his debt-to-income ratio, even though he had over six figures of outstanding student debt. The underwriters had not made the same mistake; they had picked it up and once a payment was calculated (standard with conventional and FHA guidelines), the loan was declined due to excessive debt-to-income ratios.

He was shocked. They were supposed to close on Thursday and move in before the weekend, and now the loan was declined and he was facing the loss of all of his earnest money, and worse, his wife and two young children would be homeless. It was a heart-wrenching story. As a father of two young children myself, I felt his pain and the pressure he was under. The story had a happy ending. It turned out I was able to qualify him on one of our physician programs and his family had their home. It was a bit later than they had hoped, but we were able to extend the settlement date, find temporary housing for a few weeks, and get his loan closed.

Up to this point, I had helped only a handful of physicians, written just a few short articles, and filmed several YouTube videos on what I'd learned and what physicians should be looking out for. It was this event that made me decide I had to expand. We had to launch a website and help more physicians and dentists who otherwise might face the same situation of last-minute decline.

By the next year, we'd launched a website and formally started a physician mortgage department. We've been very fortunate to have been able to help a lot of great physician clients. However, I recognize we can't process everyone's loan and I thought it was important to get this information in the hands of as many physicians aspiring to have a flawless home purchase experience as possible. I hope that will be the result of your reading this book!

WHAT ARE THE DANGER ZONES?

It's important that you understand the challenges that nearly all physicians face at three specific junctures in their career: I call these junctures "danger zones," because it is during these transitional periods when most loans are declined, due to multiple changes in the

INTRODUCTION

client's financial situation. It is when you are in one of these danger zones that it is most important for you to work with a loan officer who specializes in physician mortgage loans.

- **Med school to residency.** This transitional period is particularly dangerous because so much change is occurring. We typically see changes with student loans coming out of deferral and often going into IBR (income-based repayment), new employment contracts, sometimes with no history of filing taxes, and little if any down payment saved, and due to the demands of a resident's schedule, we're often asked to close before the first day on the job with no pay stubs in hand. A loan officer who specializes in physician home loans should be able to advise you and offer solutions to all of these challenges.

- **From residency or fellowship to attending physician.** The second danger zone is the transition to attending physician. This is an exciting time, again, with a lot of change. After two decades of education, residency, and very hard work, you are about to likely see your income increase four- or fivefold. Many of our clients have pinched pennies and clipped coupons every step of the way, and are beyond excited to be able to provide a safe home for their family. Problems can arise at this stage again, due to student loans transitioning to full repayment, or a limited down payment, often coming from gifts or sign-on bonuses, and to top it off, most clients want to close on their home when they relocate and before their first day on the new job. Again, an experienced physician loan officer will anticipate these challenges and help you navigate them safely.

- **Attending physician going into private practice.** The last danger zone where physician home loans can really come undone is when a physician is going into private practice, joining a group as a partner, or taking a position as an independent contractor receiving 1099 income (we see this a lot with anesthesiologists and emergency medicine physicians). Conventional and FHA loans, which make up 95 percent of the mortgages in the entire country, require a two-year history of self-employment or 1099 independent contractor taxes before that income can be used to qualify for a home loan. Physician mortgages, on the other hand, will generally allow qualification after zero to six months on the job, depending on the specifics of the employment contract and practice arrangement.

ABOUT THE AUTHOR

I am a fourth-generation real estate investor and landlord of about 100 rental units in Salt Lake City, Utah, co-owned and managed with my wife, Hillary, and mother, Cynthia Hale. I decided to enter the mortgage lending business about 12 years ago when, on the eve of the purchase of an eight-unit apartment building, I was called into the lender's office and informed that the loan I was approved for would have a seven percent rate instead of a five percent rate, and the down payment would be 30 percent instead of 20 percent. Since the very beginning of my career in mortgage lending, I've had a voracious appetite to help clients with transparent and honest advice.

CHAPTER ONE

THE RENT-VERSUS-BUY CONUNDRUM

You might very well be better off renting than buying. It's something you should consider carefully before you go any further down the path of buying a home. I can name a half-dozen physician clients and friends who have taken six-figure losses and two who have taken seven-figure losses, buying right at the top of the market, before the real estate and mortgage meltdown of 2006–2007. That's a pretty big hole to dig yourself out of, regardless of your income bracket. Of the two doctors who took seven-figure losses, one had to file for bankruptcy and lost the home to foreclosure, and the other has spent the last five years trying to pay down the balance to where the market is today so he can refinance out of his adjustable rate mortgage.

Buying a home is a serious decision that warrants thoughtful consideration about where you are going to be in the future and if you are willing to be a landlord if the market takes a nose dive.

I love real estate. It's in my blood as a fourth-generation apartment and rental property owner. I bought my first home when I was 20 years old and sold it three years later with a $68k tax-free gain that I rolled into my next home, a beautiful Tudor-style home on a street lined with tall trees in one of my favorite neighborhoods in Utah. I'm proud to still own that home today as a positive cash flowing rental.

I've watched my great-grandparents pass on a seven-figure inheritance. My grandparents and my mother will likely leave similar inheritances to their children, all a result of holding land and apartments throughout their lifetimes.

I plan to use those same lessons to grow and pass down a substantial net worth and positive monthly cash flow to my two children, Zander and Aria. So, for me, the choice has always been to buy, rent out, and hold for as long as humanly possible, hopefully, until it's passed on through my family trust to my children.

But what if you are not a fourth-generation landlord and you don't have the experience and knowledge I have learned from my forefathers? Then I recommend you take some time to consider the following questions:

1. Where is the real estate market today where you are buying? Does it feel frantically hot, with everybody in a panic to buy before prices go up? That is probably not the safest market to be buying into. As Warrant Buffett so famously said, "Be fearful when others are greedy and greedy when others are fearful."

2. How long do you plan to keep the property? Time forgives all in real estate! My mother and I joke about all the mistakes we have made and are thankful that even if we bought at the top, as long as we have positive cash flow and hold the property, eventually, appreciation will save us from our ignorance.

3. Will your income allow you to cover the payment if you are relocated or have to change employers? Buying

too much home is often the mistake that ends up biting young physicians early in their careers. Again, careful consideration of how much home you need and where you might be in three to five years is prudent.

I'm passionate about real estate and its wealth-building potential. I love being in control of my retirement and being able to go, see, and touch my investments. I'm also realistic and honest about the risks involved. Before buying a home, I hope you consider these personal questions and seek guidance from a wise and trusted family member, friend, or advisor who can give you perspective. If you decide it's the right choice for you and your family, then keep reading; I have a lot more to share with you!

PROBLEMS AND CHALLENGES PHYSICIANS FACE WHEN BUYING A HOME

So, you're a medical student or physician and the next step in your medical career requires you to relocate your family. You need to find a good home in a safe area, near where you will be working. Finding a rental near the university or hospital that also fits your family's needs is often difficult, as many areas around hospitals and universities are highly sought after and relatively few rentals are available, not to mention that in many areas of the country the cost of rent is more than a mortgage payment.

There are, basically, two strategies you can choose from when house hunting. Strategy number one is to look for a home first. As you are looking, you find one that piques your interest. You find out there are competing offers already on the home. The home is perfect and you want to write an offer in a hurry. Your Realtor says, "Great. You need a preapproval letter before you can submit an offer." You say, "Oh boy, I hadn't gone there yet because I wasn't certain that I wanted to buy, but now we love this home." You find yourself in a pickle because you have not gone down the path of getting preapproved in a competitive market. Many parts of the country are a seller's market, and your offer won't even be considered unless there is a preapproval letter in the file. In today's market, I'm seeing many sellers who want to talk to the loan officer to see what really has been done with that preapproval. Often, a well-priced home in a desirable neighborhood will receive multiple offers and you'll need to close quickly, which is virtually impossible if you've not already gone through a thorough preapproval and turned in all income and down payment documents for approval.

Strategy number two, which I recommend, whether you're truly looking to buy a home or just toying with the idea, is to go through the pre-underwriting process first. For doctors in today's post-mortgage-meltdown world, a preapproval really isn't enough. You should be fully credit and income approved by an underwriter, which I will touch on in more depth in the following chapters.

Once you find a home you really love, you want to be able to act decisively and move forward quickly (which sellers really love). You will not be able to do that if you haven't gone down the path of credit and income approval. I can tell you, from doing hundreds of these transactions, that you significantly reduce the amount of stress you feel by getting the credit and income approval out of the way early. Going through the preapproval process after you've put earnest money down—which may or may not be refundable—paying for inspections, appraisals, and various other due diligence expenses, while in the process of packing up your family and relocating, is incredibly stressful. If you find out that you don't qualify for a loan early in the process, you still have plenty of time to find yourself a rental. Do yourself a huge favor and get a thorough credit and income approval (more details on credit and income approval versus preapproval later) as early in the process as possible.

COMMON CHALLENGES

Particularly when physicians are just starting their careers, we see many of the same challenges in obtaining financing.

1. Large Student Loans

The first question I ask a client seeking mortgage financing is, "Do you have any student loans?" The majority of residents, fellows, and young attending physicians are going to say yes. Very few, maybe one in 50, make it out debt free. It's typical to see student loan debts somewhere in the neighborhood of $150,000 to $250,000, although I have seen physician clients with $500,000 or more in student loans—yikes! Your student loans, which are only the first things we're going to have to deal with, will likely preclude you from taking a conventional loan through Fannie Mae or Freddie Mac. This is because the Fannie Mae and Freddie Mac guidelines require that underwriting qualifies you at 2 percent of the outstanding student loan balance as a monthly payment for any student loan in deferment or showing zero payments at time of application.

For instance, let's say you graduated from med school and are going into residency. You will have a salary of $50,000 a year. You have $200,000 in student loans, so that's $4,000 a month that underwriting is going to count against your debt-to-income ratio, regardless of whether the loans are in deferment or forbearance. That puts you near a 100 percent debt-to-income ratio with student loans alone, so you are not going to qualify for a conventional loan under conventional guidelines. Know right away that you're going to need some sort of a physician home loan to exclude those deferred payments.

2. Want to Be in the New Home Prior to Starting Work

Another common challenge is if you want to move into your home prior to starting your job. Most clients generally need to close before starting work because of their intense schedules. Virtually none of our clients want to move their family twice. It is an incredible inconvenience, especially when you have children and you're trying to get them adjusted to a new school, new friends, and so on. Most physician loan programs will allow you to close prior to your start date.

3. Little to No Down Payment

It is rare that a resident, fellow, or newly attending physician will have a 20 percent down payment. I just don't see that a lot. Physician loans generally offer higher loan-to-value financing, in some cases as much as 100 percent, with no mortgage insurance, so additional savings can be achieved and the loan is easier to qualify for.

4. Added Complexity and Stresses

Many of our physician clients aren't fully aware of the added complexities and stresses on them. All they know and understand is their particular situation. As I look at a broad spectrum of clients, I see the circumstances surrounding most physicians: testing, licensing, student loans coming in and out of deferral, relocation, and new employment, to name just a few. As a student, you've likely been living on a low income, packed into a 900-square-foot apartment. You've been studying, going to school, working massive hours, trying to be a wife or a husband, trying to finance your student loan debt, and trying to pass your board exam so you can actually go on to practice. With all that is going on in your world, packing a stressful home-loan process on top of it can be too much to bear.

The easiest way to reduce stress in buying a home is to go through the underwriting process as early as possible and avoid compacting it all in the last 30 days before your move. The goal is to get all your financial documents in order, all the pieces of the puzzle put together so that you are already qualified and pre-underwritten once you find a home. Then, all that is left to do is the title search and appraisal. You're pretty much coasting to the closing table from there.

WHAT CRITERIA SHOULD I USE TO CHOOSE A MORTGAGE LENDER?

It is paramount that you work with a mortgage professional specialized in your unique situation, just as it is important to go to an expert who specializes in your medical condition. In other words, I would not go to an orthopedic surgeon if I had a heart problem. The orthopedic surgeon may be able to give me a general diagnosis and tell me that I need a heart specialist, but he's not going to be able to diagnose and treat me on the same level as a cardiologist would.

This is also true with a loan officer, but the importance of choosing the right specialist is not so obvious in the mortgage world. For example, when you visit a Realtor who tells you the best loan officer on the face of the earth is Bob, that's probably at least partially true. Bob is probably a fantastic loan officer, but if Bob, the best loan officer in the world, is not dealing with physicians all the time, he's going to miss something. Loan officers who have no experience with physicians are not going to know every solution. They're not going to know every pitfall, and they're not going to be able to guide you through the transaction and into the closing without having a bit of a learning curve.

I don't want an orthopedic surgeon going through a learning curve, figuring out why my heart's not working. You don't want a loan officer going through the learning curve on what rules and underwriting guidelines apply to student loans, down payments, sign-on or relocation bonuses, and closing before you have your first paycheck stub from your new position.

When interviewing a mortgage lender, simply ask, "How many physician clients have you worked with in the past 30 days?" If the lender says, "None," I would raise an eyebrow. If you were to ask, "How many physicians have you worked with in the past year?" and the answer is "One or two," follow that up with, "Tell me about those clients," and "May I see a testimonial or contact them?" It is your right and your responsibility to do your due diligence in asking those very intelligent and blunt questions. An answer such as, "I worked with one physician, I think, last May," doesn't cut it. The answer you're looking for is, "We've worked with several physicians in the past month. We received testimonials from 27 physicians over the past 12 months. They're all up on our site, and you can contact anyone you'd like."

HOW TO NAVIGATE THROUGH THE MANY MORTGAGE PRODUCTS ON THE MARKET

Finding the right mortgage product is confusing, and it's always changing, never static. The advice I have for you is to invest a little time and do some research. You can find a lot of information online, including physician testimonials, and so on. There's a fantastic website for physicians called WhiteCoatInvestor.com that is managed by Dr. James M. Dahle, the full-time practicing physician who wrote the foreword to this book. I was lucky enough to work on a home loan for him a couple of years ago. He started his WhiteCoatInvestor.com website because he got burned in a financial services transaction and decided that he was going to go be the Clark Kent (my term, not his) of financial investments for physicians. He does legitimate research and then writes great articles to guide his colleagues. He has covered home loan transactions and whether it is a wise decision to rent or buy at different junctures in a physician's career. His perspective and content is awesome. I'd recommend that you visit his site and check out his new book titled *The White Coat Investor: A Doctor's Guide to Personal Finance and Investing.*

After you've done as much research as you can, the next step is to select a few mortgage lenders who look as if they specialize in working with physicians. Get them on the phone and walk through your scenario in detail with them. Ask them thoughtful questions, and if you feel there is a level of trust there, ask for advice. If you give it some effort, you can and will find a loan officer who has the heart of a teacher and acts as an advisor. That's really what you are looking for: someone you believe is advising you, not selling you something. Allow that loan officer to give you the pros and cons of each loan program and help you analyze the costs and benefits. After speaking with a few people, you will quickly get a feel for who the real deal is and who has a deep understanding of your situation and the lending solutions you need.

―――― CHAPTER 2 ――――

WHERE DO I START? FIND A REALTOR OR A LOAN OFFICER?

The post-mortgage-meltdown world of mortgage underwriting is surprisingly unforgiving and, as such, catches some clients by surprise when financing problems arise. This is *especially* true for physicians, who have added complexity due to student loan debts, new employment arrangements, relocation, becoming an independent contractor, or going into private practice. You should *always* start the home-buying process by qualifying for a loan *before* working with a Realtor.

Why qualify for a loan first? This is important for several reasons:

- Conventional underwriting guidelines in the post-mortgage-meltdown world are very rigid, and the slightest issue can be a reason for decline by underwriting. There is very little room for common sense; it's done by the book and down to the letter. If you don't fit the "box," chances are your loan application will be declined.

- Without going through the qualifying process, you don't precisely know what you can qualify for and how much cash down payment you will need to part with.

- Nice homes that are in good areas and priced right sell fast, which means if you want to compete for these homes, you need to be prepared to make an offer and close quickly, sometimes in weeks, not months. Without having already started the loan process, this can be almost impossible, especially if you have new employment, student loans, and changing circumstances that affect the underwriting of your loan. Many of our clients have moved so many times the last few years that they don't even know where half of their loan documents are—in a box somewhere, no doubt. But when you have a busy work schedule and you commit to a two-week close on a home and you've not started to locate your taxes and W-2s or have yet to apply for deferment or IBR on your loans, your situation can get stressful. I recommend getting all of that out of the way up front, to eliminate this unneeded stress.

WHY PREAPPROVAL IS *NOT* ENOUGH!

If there is one thing that you'll get out of this book, I hope it is a deeper understanding of the challenges physicians, especially young physicians, face early in their career when trying to qualify for a home mortgage. I advise my clients that prequalifying is just *not* enough and I recommend they obtain a full credit and income approval prior to falling in love with a home and writing an offer.

So what's the difference between a preapproval and a credit and income approval? Preapproval is fine for the simple borrower, who is usually much easier to underwrite. If you work at Walmart and you make $13.50 an hour, 40 hours a week, fine. The chances are that a preapproval might be enough. You don't have large student loans. You have a set hourly rate or annual salary, and you are not moving

WHERE DO I START? FIND A REALTOR OR A LOAN OFFICER?

your family across the country to start a new job. So, you complete a quick online application showing you have good credit, have been at the same job for two years, and receive a W-2 salary for $28,000 a year. Preapproved. It's as easy as that. Congratulations! You fit the box.

Physicians always seem to have more moving pieces: new employment, student loans, relocations, and jumbo loan sizes all add complexity, which equals more potential pitfalls. You don't want to work through documenting and getting underwriting approval on all these issues after you have a home under contract and you've started loading up the kids in the U-Haul.

Credit and income approval starts with an application online or over the phone, then you also submit all of the documents that underwriting will need to sign off and close your loan, including transcripts if you are just coming out of medical school, two years of tax returns and W-2s, your new employment contract or offer letter, your source of down payment, and explanation as to what's happening with your student loans if they are transitioning between IBR or deferment and regular repayment. All of these items can greatly affect your loan application being approved or declined. It's my advice to not only have them reviewed by your loan officer but also *insist* that they are reviewed by an underwriter (the gatekeeper of the money) and ask for a fully underwritten credit and income approval.

Once you have a credit and income approval, you've eliminated 99 percent of the things that can and do go wrong in the loan process. You also have a *much* more attractive offer to present when you find your new home. You're not just preapproved by some gun-slinging loan officer; you've been underwriter approved. It's basically a blank check at that point. Find a home that appraises well and you are done!

SIX THINGS TO DO WHEN SEARCHING FOR A MORTGAGE LENDER

1. Obtain your credit report and FICO (Fair Isaac Company) score.

The first thing you should do in preparation for the home-buying process is to start monitoring your credit. Start three to six months before you want to close on your new home to make sure nothing slipped through the cracks. By 'nothing,' I am mostly referring to your student loans. Most physicians have several student loans through different servicers. In the shuffle or transfer of student loans, errors can and do appear on the credit report and it can be difficult to obtain information. If you are consolidating your loans, or the servicers themselves are transferring, it can be painfully slow to get things updated and the process can take months. If you've moved and missed a notice because it went to your old address, the loan servicer can report you late. You may not even know that until you pull your credit report. Fixing this error can take three to six months, so don't wait until you have 30 days to close on a home to get this done. You can pull your credit directly through the credit bureaus (I suggest you pull Experian, Transunion, and Equifax, because they are not always the same) or through your mortgage lender if you have already started the relationship.

2. Start your search for a mortgage professional, using a referral or doing an online search for "physician home loans" and the state you're moving to, or at USPhysicianHomeLoans.com.

Using a referral from a colleague, financial planner, Realtor, or the institution you are going to work for is a good place to start. If you don't know anybody, your workplace doesn't have a referral, and your financial planner doesn't have a referral in the area where you're headed, do an online search. It's really easy. You just Google "physician home loans Arizona" or wherever you're going to be practicing. Within five minutes, you should be able to compile a list of several lenders who specialize in physician home loans. This a good place to start your due diligence in finding a loan officer, but this is just your first step.

3. Contact a few lenders.

Talk to them, ask them questions, and tell them a little about your situation. It's likely as you start up your conversations with a few loan officers that one of them will immediately have a deeper understanding of your situation and be able to talk physician language, so to speak.

Be aware that once your loan hits underwriting, it may be more complex or more problematic than others. Tell the loan officer what unique situations you have. Be very honest and specific. Let the loan officer know your down payment's coming from your dad, you're relocating, you have kids. It's going to be stressful. You want to make sure that when you arrive at your new location, you'll be ready to close and move the family into your new home. Talk through your situation and what you think might be the challenges and then allow the mortgage professional to respond and offer advice.

Good mortgage professionals, the physician mortgage experts, will understand IBR and student loans. They will ask about your new employment contract and whether it's based on salary or production. You'll find that they understand and describe your situation even better than you do, because they have guided clients through this before and they ask questions that you haven't thought about. These are all good signs that you are dealing with someone who has worked with physicians in the past. You want to connect with someone like that to start going down the credit- and income-approval process.

4. Check your loan officer's reputation.

Selecting the right professional loan officer is a big decision. You're about to risk money and the mental sanity of your family as you relocate across the country to your new home, and you have a lot at risk. Do your due diligence: ask the hard questions, study the mortgage professional online, and make sure he or she is an expert. If you are not sure, ask for the names and numbers of the last three physicians the mortgage professional worked with. If the mortgage professional balks, he or she is not the expert you are looking for. Move on and keep looking.

You can check mortgage professionals' reputations through a couple of sources. I would recommend you Google their name and always ask for past physician client testimonials. I think that is very important, because you get a feel for not only what the loan officer says but also the viewpoint of their clients who have gone through the process. Those former clients have firsthand experience of the lenders' level of service.

A loan is more than just rate. It is about whether that loan professional can get you the loan product he or she has promised to deliver without driving you mad. For instance, one way a loan professional can drive you mad is by asking at the very last moment for a bank statement or a W-2 from two years ago that's at your parents' house somewhere. That's not what you want to hear when everything's packed in the U-Haul and you're supposed to move your family into your new home tomorrow.

Consider two things:

- the level of service, communication, and responsiveness of the mortgage professional during the transaction

- the ability of that professional to get you into your home seamlessly

The level of service can't be measured through a good-faith estimate. The only way you can measure it is through the experience of the clients the mortgage professional has served. So check the mortgage professional's reputation, check testimonials, and ask to talk to past clients if need be.

5. Organize your financial documents.

Have two years of tax returns or school transcripts (if in school within the past 24 months) available, your new employment contract or offer letter (signed or unsigned), information on your student loans servicer(s), source of down payment, and anything else you think prudent or unique to your situation.

You want to move toward a full credit and income approval. Loan officers in different areas of the country may not use that exact term, but I would recommend that you insist on your documents getting all the way to the underwriting level. That's the safest approach to make sure you're not going to have a problem or be surprised when you're relocating across the country.

6. Notify the loan officer of any changes in income, job status, or credit.

This is *huge*! Don't change anything once you have your credit and income approval. Be disgustingly thrifty before you close on your home. Afterward, take the vacation and buy the furniture, if you must.

If there are changes, notify your lender right away. Anything that changes your income, liabilities, or credit can affect your approval. For example, if your employment start date changes or if you decide to take a vacation and put the cost on a zero-interest Discover card, talk to your lender. Do not try to hide any financial or employment changes, as this will likely come back to bite you at the last minute. Once you have that credit and income approval, you should lock down your credit. Don't make any major purchases and don't open any new accounts or close any old ones. Your mindset should be, "I'm currently approved and I am not doing anything until I'm in my home."

HOW TO FIND AN AWESOME REALTOR

Finding a capable Realtor who understands your unique needs is a critical yet challenging part of the home-buying process. I've seen Realtors execute a client's transaction perfectly, and I've seen some of them totally mess it up. Here, I will describe what defines a capable Realtor from the perspective of an intermediary between the Realtor and the buyer, and why there is no room for error.

TIP:
Choose a Realtor who has physician and/or family relocation experience.

I would advise you to find a Realtor who is familiar with either physicians or relocation, because he or she will understand that there are additional details for consideration and added repercussions if contract dates are not executed flawlessly. This is not as important for those who are not relocating from another state. If the closing moves a week one way or the other, it's not that big of a deal. You just extend your lease another month or you have an extra week to move out of your current home before you move into the new home. But when you're relocating across the country, there's no margin for error.

Your Realtor should understand the complexities and be experienced with client relocations. For example, let's say that the home you're buying is part of a chain of transactions. So, you're buying a home from a seller who is buying a new home, and maybe that other seller is also buying another home. Somewhere in the chain, if someone's loan goes awry, everyone may well have to put on the brakes and wait for that person's loan to go through. That's a real problem if you, your spouse, and your four kids plan to unload the U-Haul over the weekend so you can start your new position on Monday. You can see how this can get ugly quickly. Where do you put six people and a U-Haul truck while you're waiting for the seller's loan to go through?

An experienced Realtor dealing with relocation should be smart enough to say to the seller's Realtor, "I represent a family. They're relocating. They've done all their due diligence. What's going on with your sellers? Are they buying a new home? And what's going to happen if their home doesn't close? What's their contingency plan?" The Realtor should be talking to the selling agent. Typically, that would happen after you've written up the offer and been accepted, but there should be some dialogue and some plans. The Realtor should know that, come hell or high water, you need to be in that home on your closing date.

Here's another example. Let's say your Realtor is not experienced in this sphere of relocation and doesn't understand the importance of making sure everything goes off without a hitch. He or she decides that you should write an offer on a short sale and tells you it's no problem because it's a bank-approved short sale. It's totally safe. Well, maybe, maybe not. Does your Realtor have the bank's short-sale approval letter in hand? Has your Realtor looked at it? Is it good through the date on which you're going to close? In other words, if you are negotiating an approved short sale and have a bank's short-sale approval letter, the bank that has the current loan on the property is accepting less than what's owed. However, if the bank says it will accept this amount through June 15 and your closing is on June 30, you will need a new approved short-sale letter, and if you apply for an extension and a new letter, the whole short-sale arrangement is back up for reconsideration. A new property evaluation may have to be done by the bank. The owner of the note may have transferred. There are a dozen things that could go wrong with that short sale closing on time. Bottom line, the Realtor handling your transaction needs to do more due diligence to be certain of the seller's situation and aware of all possible delays before committing you to a home closing timeline.

HOW TO BUY A NEW HOME A LONG WAY FROM HOME

Many times when you're a remote buyer, you're going to be handling the inspections remotely. This means that the Realtor's going to work or act on your behalf, meeting with the inspector, talking with the inspector about the issues, sending you the report, and being your eyes and ears. The Realtor also needs to be at your disposal when you come to town to house hunt. When you're relocating, you're going to have one, maybe two, visits to the state and you're probably only going to be there for a couple of days. You're going to want to do intense house hunting, perhaps eight to ten hours a day looking for houses and getting familiar with the areas, and you're going to need major help, often on a weekend.

If the Realtor is a one-person shop, has two kids, and doesn't like to work on weekends and that's the only time when you're available to house hunt, that's a real conflict. So, you want to make sure that the Realtor has a staff or is willing to put the weekend, or week day(s), on hold when you come into town, because you mean business and you've got to get your house hunting done.

One more important detail not to be overlooked by the Realtor is the potential for a remote closing when you are not likely to be in the state where the home is on the closing date. This will be discussed later in the book. But let's say you are living in Virginia and buying a home in Utah. If you're working with Joe Schmoe Realtor, who has done one or two transactions, chances are he's not going to think through the complexities of getting documents across the country and back to meet your deadlines. If he's adept in relocations and experienced in working with physicians, this is par for the course. It will be ingrained in his head to ask, "Where are you going to be when we close?" And he's going to be able to write your purchase agreement and navigate the closing process flawlessly for you.

CHAPTER 3

THE PHYSICIAN HOME LOAN

HOW CAN I FIND A PHYSICIAN HOME LOAN LENDER IN MY CITY?

The number-one mortgage question doctors ask is, "How can I find a physician home loan lender in my city?"

Google It

I've mentioned this before, but it bears repeating: Google "physician home loans" plus the area where you are looking to buy. Mortgage professionals who specialize in working with physicians have written articles, blogged about their business, or have posted testimonials from physicians, which will come up in response to your search.

Visit USPhysicianHomeLoans.com. This website is basically a directory and provides a map of the United States, and each state has a hot button. If you click on Arizona, a box will come up with the name of the bank that offers physician home loans in Arizona, the contact information for the loan officer, and a brief general description of the bank's services and program guidelines. The website does not provide interest rates.

WHAT IS THE DIFFERENCE BETWEEN A PHYSICIAN HOME LOAN AND A CONVENTIONAL LOAN?

In the simplest terms, a physician home loan will have more liberal underwriting guidelines, whereas a conventional loan is underwritten to more rigid and intransigent guidelines.

The Conventional Loan

When we talk about conventional loans, we're talking about loans that are purchased by Fannie Mae and Freddie Mac. More than 95 percent of the loans in the USA are currently purchased by Fannie Mae, Freddie Mac, or Ginnie Mae, and are conventional, VA, or FHA loans.

So, it doesn't matter which bank you go to. The banks (Wells, Chase, Bank of America, etc.) generally retain the servicing of these loans, billing every month, collecting payments, administering escrow accounts, managing taxes and insurance, and providing a written payoff statement when the loan is to be paid off. That's all they do, in most cases. They don't actually own the loan anymore; they just get a premium for servicing it.

The loan itself is put together with a bunch of other loans that are similar to yours and then sold to Fannie Mae and Freddie Mac, which in turn bundle them and sell them as mortgage-backed securities (bonds secured by mortgages) on Wall Street. Because Fannie and Freddie are government-sponsored enterprises, making loans from coast-to-coast, they have to have sweeping, uncompromising guidelines in order to maintain consistency in the kind of loans that are delivered to them. In doing so, they usually deliver the lowest interest rate. But in order to qualify for a conventional loan, your situation has to match their rigid guidelines exactly, or fit inside the "box," as we call it. So, a physician home loan is not a loan that is likely to be sold to Fannie Mae or Freddie Mac.

The Physician Home Loan

Typically, a physician home loan is a portfolio loan product, meaning that the bank or institution that is making the loan is actually going to keep the loan and retain the servicing of the loan. Since the bank is keeping the loan, it can make judgment calls in underwriting and assessing risk and can, therefore, take a more liberal approach with physicians than it would for other people, because it deems physicians less likely to default on the loan.

There are several typical benefits of a physician home loan over a conventional loan:

- **Higher chance of approval.** Physicians with outside-the-box or complicated situations are more likely to be approved for a physician home loan than for a conventional loan.

- **Low down payment.** The physician home loan will finance higher loan to values, in some cases as much as 100 percent of the purchase price.

- **No mortgage insurance.** I don't know of any physician home loan that includes mortgage insurance. This is a huge savings. Let's say you are buying a $350,000 home and want to put 5 percent down on a conventional loan. Depending on your credit score, where your home is located, and a few other factors, your mortgage insurance is somewhere around 1 percent. Buying a $350,000 home means you're going to be paying about $3,500 a year in mortgage insurance. Over 10 years, that's $35,000 in mortgage insurance that you would have to pay with a conventional loan, and which, conversely, you would save with a physician home loan.

- **Student loan(s) can be excluded from your debt-to-income ratio.** This is a significant difference between a physician home loan and a conventional loan, and is particularly valuable for someone transitioning from med school into residency. This is discussed further in the next section.

- **Higher loan limits.** Because physician home loans don't sell to Fannie and Freddie and are not a conventional product, they are not going to have conventional loan limits. The loan limits will vary based on your geographical area and the institution that's making the loan. Typically, you'll be able to borrow a higher amount and put less money down with a physician home loan than you would with a conventional loan.

- **Ability to close before starting work.** This is a considerable benefit of a physician home loan. Most conventional mortgage lenders will require that you have two paycheck stubs before you close on your new home. A physician home loan will typically allow you to close prior to starting your new position, based on your employment contract or offer letter. Some programs will allow you to close as far out as 120 days before your start date, while others will require you to close within 30 days. Make sure to check the exact closing guidelines with your loan officer.

- **Flexibility on proof of income, enabling earlier home purchase.** Conventional underwriting guidelines typically require two years' worth of tax returns for proof of income if you are an independent contractor. Emergency medicine physicians and anesthesiologists, who are commonly 1099 contractors, would fit in this type of employment arrangement. Some physician home loan programs will allow a 1099 or self-employed physician to qualify with an income history of as little as zero to six months. So, you could buy a home almost two years earlier with a physician loan than you could with a conventional loan. Again, this will vary, based on your lender's guidelines and how your employment contract is written.

One more intangible benefit of the physician home loan is the people who are helping you with the loan: the loan originator, processor, and underwriter. If they're in the business of administering physician home loans, they'll understand your potentially more complex circumstances. You're likely going to be dealing with people who are more specialized and have seen everything you're going to throw at them, and its probable the experience of moving through the loan is going to be more enjoyable and less stressful.

PHYSICIAN HOME LOAN FAQS

You can find the answers to these and other frequently asked questions on our website at www.UtahPhysicianHomeLoans.com/videos.

Do Physician Home Loans Have Higher Closing Costs Than Conventional Loans?

Yes. In most cases, closing costs and interest rate are slightly higher than compared to a conventional loan. Keep in mind a physician loan will have more liberal guidelines, such as a higher loan-to-value ratios and higher loan amounts, and, therefore, take on a little more risk. As such, there are less of these type of loans out there, and the lending institutions offering them want a slightly higher return. Whenever possible, we try to get our clients into a conventional loan first, though it's not possible in many cases, due to one or more of the factors we've discussed in the previous chapters. The good news is that the physician loan is going to be in the ballpark with the conventional loan. On average, you can count on it being comparable within 1/2 percent in rate and 1 percent in closing costs.

Why Does the Physician Home Loan Cost More?

Conservatively, some 120 hours of work go into the average physician home loan, once you include the loan originators work, the processing, underwriting, all the auxiliary staff, compliance, disclosures, closing, and the funding department. An amazing number of people are required to get a loan from application to closing today, with all the new legal compliance, disclosures, and government regulation. Those people all have to be paid. They all require a building above their heads, lights, air conditioning, and coffee in the morning. It takes money to make those 120 hours happen.

With a conventional loan, there are two ways that a loan officer and lending institution, can be compensated:

1. Up-front fees or closing costs that can be paid by you, the borrower, or by the seller of the home if you have negotiated seller-paid closing costs. These usually include an origination fee, which is customarily one percent of the loan amount and which can be thought of as the profit in the loan for the lending institution and loan officer; an underwriting fee of usually $600 to $800, which goes toward paying the underwriters for underwriting the loan; and a processing fee, which is usually between $250 and

$500 and goes to pay the processor who's processing the loans.

2. Alternatively, the costs can be covered via a higher interest rate. Let's say your loan officer could lock 4.5 percent today and would need to charge all those standard fees listed above. Well, if you're fine with 4.625 or 4.75 percent, your lender doesn't have to charge all those fees. He or she can say, "Hey, I have a low closing-cost option and I don't charge an origination fee. My rate is 4.625 percent." That means, each year, you're going to pay an extra 1/8 percent interest over the life of your loan. Over 30 years, that means you're paying an extra 3.75 percent in total interest. You will pay 3.75 percent more in interest over 30 years to save 1 percent up front. Maybe this option makes sense, maybe it doesn't. If you're likely going to be moving in a couple of years, it can make sense to save the 1 percent in closing costs up front. If you're going to be there until you die or keep it as a rental after you move, it doesn't make sense. With a conventional loan, you have the latitude to either set up the loan as a fee structure paid at closing or as a rate structure, wherein you agree to a higher rate but lower costs and potentially less cash out of pocket up front.

With a physician home loan, loan officers usually don't have the ability to move the interest rate up and take compensation via rate. They must charge the hour-costs up front, so you're more commonly going to see processing, underwriting, and origination fees charged as up-front closing costs.

How Will My Student Loans Affect a Physician Home Loan?

The answer depends on where you are in your career and what your student loan plan is. If you are a med student going into residency, you are likely to have student loans that are in deferral or forbearance. If you're applying for a conventional loan, the conventional underwriting guidelines state that you have to qualify with 2 percent of the outstanding balance of your loan as a monthly payment. So if you have $250,000 in deferred student loans and zero repayments so far, conventional guidelines require that you qualify with 2 percent of that, which is $5,000 a month. If your residency salary is $48,000 a year, or $4,000 a month, you're not going to qualify for any mortgage, because underwriting is already calculating you have a 125 percent debt-to-income ratio with the student loan debt alone.

A physician home loan program does not follow those guidelines. It allows you to either document what your future IBR payments will be, or document that you can continue to defer those loans throughout your residency and/or fellowship. The physician home loan programs apply common sense to underwriting, allowing you to qualify when conventional loans will not.

If you're moving to an attending position and your student loans have been in IBR and are reporting as such, both conventional and physician loans will likely assess your qualification based on the IBR payment amount. If your credit report shows a zero payment, both types of loan will likely verify and qualify you, based on what your actual student loan repayment amount will be. The physician loan may still behoove you in this situation, as it will allow you to use the income from your pending employment contract, which, in most cases, will be enough to cover the student loan and mortgage payments.

INCOME-BASED REPAYMENT (IBR)

Income-based repayment, or IBR, was created to ensure that student loan payments don't push you into bankruptcy when you're getting your career started. Basically, your payment will be based on 15 percent of your discretionary income, which depends on how many dependents you have and a few other factors. You can find a bunch of IBR calculators online to help you determine whether you might qualify for the program. However, many of them are confusing. We use http://www.ibrinfo.org/calculator.php. It's simple. You answer six questions, and it calculates your payment.

How Does IBR Affect Qualifying for a Physician Home Loan?

IBR may make the difference between qualifying and not qualifying for a home loan, but it depends on where you are in your career. If you are a graduating medical student with deferred student loans that will be going into IBR after your payment grace period is up, then those student loan payments will likely report as a zero payment on your credit report. Conventional underwriting guidelines will not recognize IBR, because it is considered a form of deferral or forbearance. So, say you are starting your residency program, going down the path of a conventional loan, and you have $150,000 in student loan debt. Even if you could prove under federal law that you qualify for IBR and your repayment is only going to be $300 a month, conventional mortgage underwriters would still qualify you, based on counting 2 percent per month of your outstanding student loan balance ($3,000) against your debt-to-income ratio. This is a deal killer for any conventional loan. Remember that the conventional loan does not allow you to qualify with any deferral, forbearance, or IBR payment. It always hits you for 2 percent of the outstanding loan balance, or the fully amortizing student loan payment, as a liability to be counted against your debt-to-income ratio.

Typically, a physician home loan will allow you to qualify based on the IBR reduced payment. So, let's say you are transitioning from residency into a fellowship. A very commonplace income situation would be the following: Sarah, who is making $50,000 a year in her last year of residency, is going into a fellowship where she will be making $85,000 a year. Her student loans have been in forbearance or deferral through residency. Now she wants to move into IBR throughout her fellowship, to keep payments manageable until she takes an attending position.

Sarah applies for a physician home loan. We run an IBR calculator based on her upcoming salary—not the $50,000 salary she had, but the $85,000 salary she is going to have as a fellow. She has $250,000 in student loans and a spouse and three kids. The calculator spits out a payment of $325 a month. Generally, physician loan underwriting guidelines are going to qualify her at a payment of $325 a month. The physician home loan underwriter is going to say, "We know you're at $85,000 a year and are only going to pay $325 a month in student loan payments under IBR until you take your attending position. We also know that your $85,000 salary is going to double or triple once you finish your fellowship, and those student loan payments are going to pop up to about $2,500 a month. We're pretty sure you can handle an extra $2,125 a month in payments when that happens. So we're going to allow you to qualify based on the IBR amount. We're applying common sense in forecasting that your payments will go up, but your overall debt-to-income ratio will go down, due to your increased salary as an attending physician."

With a physician loan, underwriting has the latitude to use common sense, which, in Sarah's case, makes the difference in qualifying for a home or being declined with a conventional loan.

Should I Pay for a Preapproval?

No. I don't know of any reputable mortgage lender anywhere who charges for a preapproval. By "preapproval," I want you to remember to insist on a full credit and income approval. It is a service that loan officers should provide to clients for free, because it's in the client and loan officer's best interest to do so. An important part of a loan officer's job is to do the due diligence of ensuring that you qualify according to the loan program's underwriting guidelines before you write an offer. Although this is time-consuming work on the part of the lender, the client should not have to pay for this service and should insist upon getting a full credit and income approval that has been sent to and reviewed by an underwriter. Charging $50 or $100 or $250 for that work is not how a loan officer should earn a living, and I would consider this a red flag.

You might be charged for a credit report, because the credit bureau is outside the control of the loan officer, but I would be very skeptical of working with someone who charges for a preapproval. You want your loan officer to provide solutions, help, and guidance, not to nickel and dime you.

What Is Included in a Good-Faith Estimate (GFE) for My Physician Loan?

This is one of the most common questions we get from clients and see in different forums that we visit. The good-faith estimate (GFE) is laid out on a government-created and required form, recently updated as part of the mortgage reforms undertaken after the mortgage meltdown. Its stated goal is to provide the consumer with greater transparency and understanding. A good-faith estimate must be provided by a U.S. mortgage lender or broker to a customer, as required by the Real Estate Settlement Procedures Act (RESPA). This applies to all mortgage lenders providing physician home loans or conventional loans. The estimate must include an itemized list of fees and costs associated with the loan and must be provided within three business days of the loan application date. These mortgage fees, also called settlement costs or closing costs, cover expenses associated with a home loan, including lender fees, appraisal, title insurance and fees, transfer taxes, and other third-party miscellaneous charges.

A good-faith estimate, which is set out on a standardized form, is intended to be used to compare offers (or quotes) from different lenders or brokers (for an example of this form see Appendix A on page 125, or visit www.UtahPhysicianHomeLoans.com/good-faith-estimate). Once a property is located and the loan officer has all your information, the loan officer has three days to issue the GFE. Once that has been done, the fees are locked down, and can't be arbitrarily changed. The loan officer will also estimate third-party fees (title, appraisals, etc.), which can only be changed by a maximum of 10 percent. The GFE forces lenders to guarantee their fees and also clearly discloses:

- if your loan is adjustable or fixed;

- if there's any prepayment penalties on your loan;

- if your interest rate is locked or floating;

- how many days your interest rate is locked.

Although the GFE is helpful in many ways, it is also lacking in a few areas:

- It does not tell you who is paying the title fees, which can vary depending where in the country you are buying. In California, for instance, who pays the title fees is negotiated as part of the purchase agreement. In Utah, it is standard in the state-approved, real-estate-purchase contract that the seller pays for the owner's title policy. This can be pretty confusing because, in Utah, your GFE will show a $2,500 owner's title policy fee but does not indicate that the seller pays this charge. The form fails to show any and all credits paid by the seller, which will vary, depending on your location and how the purchase agreement was negotiated.

- It does not show your total payment. It shows whether your monthly payment will include taxes and insurance, but it doesn't show how much your total payment is with taxes, insurance, and homeowners association fees. Most people want to know what their payment is going to be, including those fees, so as to not be surprised on the day of closing.

- It doesn't show monthly mortgage insurance amounts if applicable.

- It doesn't show if you made a deposit up front with the seller or builder.

- It doesn't itemize where every dollar of your closing costs are going and to whom. It just shows you lump sum totals of closing costs.

- It doesn't show whether the seller has agreed to pay any of your closing costs. The GFE may list $12,000 in closing costs, but $3,000 of that may be from the seller's proceeds to cover the owner's title policy. Per your purchase agreement, the seller may agree to pay part or all of the remaining $9,000 of your closing costs. So, the total amount you end up actually having to come up with at closing can be quite different from what is disclosed on the GFE.

Because the GFE leaves out some key information, such as total monthly payment and cash to close, which is likely the most important information to you, most loan officers have something called a fees worksheet (for an example of this form see Appendix B on page 131, or visit www.UtahPhysicianHomeLoans.com/fees-worksheet). Some loan officers call it a financing proposal. The fees worksheet, or financing proposal, is a more detailed document that shows a total payment with taxes, insurance, mortgage insurance (if applicable), total amount of cash needed to close, and all of the credits that may be coming to you.

Shopping for a home loan based on GFEs is difficult, because a lender will not usually issue a GFE until you have identified a property. Once the lender issues a GFE, it's a guarantee. Lenders can't guarantee the GFE if they don't know when buyers are going to close, what the loan amount is, and what the purchase price is. When shopping for a home loan, consider asking for a fees worksheet or a financing proposal that clearly itemizes all costs and all credits.

Can I Get a Construction Loan with a Physician Home Loan?

Yes. In some areas of the country, there are lenders who will approve a construction loan based on the physician lender's long-term loan approval. Typically, the construction loan itself is used to purchase the lot and build the home. It is a short-term loan (3 to 12 months usually) and must be paid off once the home is built. Once the home is complete, you will refinance into your physician home loan, generally, a 15-year or 30-year fixed loan, which will pay off the construction loan.

The construction loan for physicians might be a harder loan to find, but it is out there. Generally, banks that offer construction loans are not in the physician loan business, but we've been successful in securing them for clients when we can issue a long-term commitment on our physician loan program. The physician home loan lender is, basically, offering a written approval to the bank making the construction loan. This written approval states that the lender has underwritten the borrower and will make the loan once the home construction is completed. Visit www.USPhysicianHomeLoans.com for a list of lenders who will offer physician construction loans.

A Physician Home Loan Versus an Adjustable Rate Mortgage (ARM): When Is an ARM the Right Product for Me?

I think of an adjustable rate mortgage as a tool, as a means to an end. Like any tool, it can be beneficial and it can be dangerous, depending on your understanding and use of it. An ARM can be a great tool for physicians, particularly if it's likely either of the following may occur:

- You will sell the home within the next five to seven years.

- Your income will increase substantially or your outgoing monthly debt will decrease substantially in the next five to seven years.

ARMs usually have a fixed period of one to ten years. If you're going to be in a three-year residency, fellowship, or attending position, likely followed by relocation, and you have no inclination to be a landlord, there's a pretty good chance you're going to sell that home in three years and you should consider an ARM.

With an ARM product, you'll have a lower interest rate, typically 1 to 1.5 percent below the 30-year fixed rate, so your carrying cost while you are in the home will be lower. Let's say that you're stretched really thin through a residency or fellowship, you make between $50,000 and $80,000 a year, you've got four kids, and you live in California. It is really hard to raise a family of six people and afford a home in California on that budget. If you know that at the end of your residency or fellowship you're going to be making a serious six-figure income, you might consider an ARM. There is certainly a risk of higher rates and payments at the end of your fixed-rate period. However, at that time it might not be that big a deal for you if your payment goes up another $300, $400, or $500 a month. Even if rates are terrible, your income is so much higher at that point that the potentially higher mortgage payment is much more manageable and not likely to kill you.

Because a rapid increase in income is not the norm for most people, ARMs are not the safest option for most homebuyers trying to qualify for a little more home. For you, the risk of going with a higher payment down the road may be less than the risk of being able to make it through the next few years on a low to moderate income. Thus, an ARM product can be especially useful to physicians who will have an increase in income in the near future.

As a side note, my general advice to young families just starting out is to be conservative in the home purchase price rather than risk an adjustable rate mortgage. This is a very personal decision, which should be considered carefully by each family.

Are Physician Home Loan Products All the Same?

From the consumer standpoint, it may seem as if there is one physician home loan and that one loan is universal across the country.

THE PHYSICIAN HOME LOAN

But that's not the case. Physician home loans are usually individual bank portfolio loan programs; the bank or the institution making the loan creates its own rules based on a common-sense approach geared toward physicians. Each bank is going to have slightly different underwriting guidelines.

In the most general terms, physician loan products are more liberal in their underwriting guidelines than conventional loans, and their benefits over conventional loans will be similar. As discussed previously, they allow for more flexibility in calculating student loan payments and potentially higher debt-to-income ratios for physicians, because they know that their income is very likely to expand in the future. They typically allow higher loan amounts and reduced down-payment requirements. I know some institutions that accommodate a purchase price of up to $1.5 million with as little as 5 percent down, whereas if you were a more traditional borrower looking for a jumbo loan like that, you would need 20 or 25 percent down. Physician home loans are also more liberal in the way they handle self-employment income, requiring fewer years of tax records.

It would be difficult to describe all the different types of products out there, because each bank's guidelines vary and frequently change. Without getting too specific about any one bank or institution's guidelines, I will say that there's more flexibility with physician home loan products. The best way to determine whether a physician home loan is right for you is to find a loan officer who is recognized in the field, has access to these products, and can give you specifics for your particular situation.

If you visit www.USPhysicianHomeLoans.com, you'll see general descriptions to give you some direction and help you narrow your search.

CHAPTER 4

HOME LOAN OPTIONS FOR THE GRADUATING MEDICAL STUDENT GOING INTO RESIDENCY

WHY RESIDENT PHYSICIANS STRUGGLE THE MOST

Of all the physicians we serve, we see residents struggle the most with mortgage financing. Residents, above all other physicians, should be 100 percent certain they are working with a loan officer who is a physician mortgage specialist. As a resident, you are likely to have the most student loan debt, make the least amount of money, have the least amount of your own money accumulated for down payment, and have the most confusing student loan situations when moving from med school to residency.

I refer to the period between graduating med school and when your student loans come out of deferral as "no man's land." I call it this for two reasons. First, it is a period of time when your student loans are likely reporting at their highest balances, but no payments show up on your credit reports. Those student loans are coming due within six months. The student loan lenders, typically, won't defer for another year, and your resident salary is rarely going to qualify you for the new mortgage payment and the fully amortized student loan payments. There are very few loan solutions for new residents looking to purchase a home while in no man's land. Loan officers and underwriters for conventional U.S. Department of Veterans Affairs (VA) and FHA home loan programs are rarely able to figure out a solution and get you closed on time.

The second reason is because most new residents want to close and move into their new homes prior to starting their grueling residency work schedule. Thus, most have hard-to-calculate student loan liabilities and no history or proof of income.

Without question, I receive more panicked calls from resident physicians who have started the loan process with another loan officer and had their loan applications declined at the last minute. This transitional period from med school to residency is a killer of mortgage applications. It's a time when you should be exceedingly careful about whom you trust to handle the financing of your new home and absolutely insist on a fully underwritten credit and income approval prior to making an offer on a home.

CASE 1

TYPICAL CHALLENGES RESIDENT PHYSICIANS FACE

Greg is a typical graduating medical student. He is married with two children and has mid- to high-700 FICO scores, $10,000 to $25,000 in savings/gift for down payment, low consumer debt, and student loans of $150,000.

Greg signed a four-year, *non-contingent contract* with a hospital in Seattle, Washington, and his residency program offers an annual salary of $54,000.

Three unique challenges Greg will face are:

- He has little money for a down payment, about 5 to 10 percent.

- He is relocating in June, and he wants to purchase as soon as he arrives and before his first day of residency so he does not have to move his young family twice.

- He has $150,000 in deferred loans that he must start to repay before the end of the year or he'll have to reapply for additional deferment or IBR.

GREG'S OPTIONS:

FHA or VA (Veteran) Home Loan

- **Down payment.** Not required with VA. FHA will allow it to be gifted, and requires no liquid assets or reserves in addition to the 3.5 percent down. Greg would have enough for a down payment with FHA or VA.

- **Closing.** Closing 30 days before employment with a two-year contract is allowed by *some* underwriters, but most will want to see at least one pay stub prior to closing. This is definitely a potential issue. Greg will want to make sure he is fully credit and income approved by underwriting prior to his making an offer, committing to a closing date, and packing the U-Haul for Seattle.

- **Student loans.** Student loans in deferment or forbearance 12-plus months from the closing date are not counted in the debt-to-income ratio for FHA or VA. However, student loans that do enter into repayment within 12 months would be factored into underwriting debt-to-income ratios. In Greg's case, as is the case with most deferred student loans, the $150,000 in student loans show up on his credit report with a balance but with no payment. In the case where they are coming due within 12 months from closing, underwriting guidelines call for 2 percent of the outstanding balance to be calculated and used against Greg's debt-to-income ratio. Therefore, underwriting will hit him for a $3,000 a month student loan payment, which will destroy his debt-to-income ratio.

Unless Greg can find a loan officer and underwriter who are very familiar with IBR and who are willing to qualify him based on his future IBR payments, FHA and VA are very unlikely to work for him. Nine out of ten FHA or VA underwriters would decline Greg's application.

Conventional Home Loan

- **Down payment.** Greg would be okay with his limited down payment, as conventional loans will allow as little as 5 percent down.

- **Closing.** Greg *might* be able to close without 30 days of pay stubs, if he finds a lender who is experienced in serving physicians. This is a gray area, which is up to underwriter discretion, and very few underwriters see enough employment contracts to be comfortable with allowing a client to close on future income. This is a major sticking point for many of the physicians who tell us they've been informed they cannot close without a full 30 days of pay stubs. Greg would definitely want an underwriter to review his employment contract and give the blessing on his closing before he started his residency position. As always,

I would suggest you cross this bridge well before you fall in love with a home and write an offer.

- **Student loans.** Student loan deferment, forbearance, and IBR are not recognized at all by conventional loans. Monthly payments based on 2 to 5 percent (depending on the lender/bank) of outstanding loan balance will be calculated into the debt-to-income ratio, making it impossible for Greg to qualify. This will kill Greg's chance of a conventional loan, because of the underwriter-calculated payment of at least $3,000 per month (2 percent of the $150,000 student loan balance).

Again, Greg's debt-to-income ratio is too high, and his loan application will likely be declined for conventional financing.

Physician Home Loan

- **Down payment.** Greg would be allowed a 0 to 5 percent down payment, depending on location and the physician lender's guidelines.

- **Closing.** Greg would be allowed to close 30 days before he starts his residency; in some cases, as much as 60 days is possible.

- **Student loans.** Greg would be allowed to exclude his deferred student loans or qualify based on future IBR payments.

The physician home loan would give Greg some peace of mind. The three challenges that are problematic with FHA and conventional loans are not challenges for the physician home loan. This doesn't mean that every resident ends up with a physician home loan, as you'll see below in Dr. Schwartz's story. Conventional home loans are, generally, the most problematic for residents and the physician home loan is more often the best choice of the three options.

HOW DO I KNOW WHICH LOAN IS TRULY THE BEST OPTION?

When I speak to relocating med students going into residency, it's vital I get a good grip on their overall situation. By asking the following detailed questions, I determine which price range of home they are looking for and the source of their down payment: How much money do you have to put down? Where is the money coming from? Is the money already in your account or is it going to be gifted or borrowed?

I ask about their student loans. How much do they have in terms of student loans? Are the loans in repayment or forbearance, and what is the plan for the loans after starting residency? Then, I would ask about the timing of their relocation: When do you wrap up med school? How much time do you have off? Will you be taking any vacations or traveling before you relocate? When do you start your residency? When do you want to be in your home?

These details are really important in order to get it right and not to miss any piece of the puzzle, which could create a last-minute blow up. Based on the answers, I would roll through the three scenarios described above. This is a very common interview or initial consultation, which I have over the phone with clients. I get to know their situation, and I try to make them aware of the challenges that they are likely to face if they aren't aware of them already. After this interview, clients will often come to their own conclusion about which loan will work best for them. When you find a loan officer who asks all the right questions and then takes the time to advise you

A TRUE STORY: DR. SCHWARTZ'S NEAR-DISASTER

Dr. Schwartz had a typical residency situation: he was young, married with two children, and had about $175,000 in student loans. He had just scraped up enough for about a 3 percent down payment, so he didn't have much liquidity or reserves (savings left after closing). He had more challenges than most, because his credit scores were a little lower. He was also buying in California, which is a common-law state where you have to take into consideration the spouse's liabilities when considering a loan. His set of circumstances was otherwise similar to that of the majority of residents we advise.

For some reason, I answered Dr. Schwartz's call after hours, which is unusual for me. (When I'm at home, I usually devote time to my kids and don't take business calls.) On the other end of the line was a very panicked young man.

Dr. Schwartz explained that his loan had just been declined and he that had already moved his family into the home. It started typically enough. He had gone through the preapproval process, received his preapproval letter, and made an offer on a great home near the hospital where his residency program was. When it came time to close the loan, the loan officer told him that they were having delays, but they would still be able to get him closed. The loan officer told him to be patient and to try to negotiate with the seller for more time before the closing.

As it turned out, the seller was going through a divorce and couldn't make the mortgage payment that month. The seller agreed to allow Dr. Schwartz to move in if he released the down payment money as nonrefundable earnest money and made a monthly payment as rent until the closing. Dr. Schwartz made the nonrefundable deposit, every dime of the money that he had saved. He was literally tapped and had nothing left until he received his first pay stub as a resident.

After Dr. Schwartz had been in the home for two weeks—his loan process had been going on for eight weeks at that time—his lender finally called and told him that his loan application had been declined due to his credit and student loan debt. Both should have been apparent to the loan officer at preapproval. Dr. Schwartz had no time, no money, and no plan or ability to move his family and find another home. As you can imagine, he was in a dead panic when he called me. He had not yet told his wife that his loan application had been declined, and he did not know where to turn.

We discussed his situation in detail and hashed out all the challenges. I told him that I thought my team could help him and I'd like to pick up the ball where the other lender left off. Fortunately, we were able to add his father as a cosigner, work through his credit issues, and get him closed, and pay off the seller within about three weeks.

This story is particularly scary but demonstrates the hazards for residents who have complicated situations and who work with traditional lenders who have no experience in serving physicians. Often, it's only after the loan is deep in underwriting that the underwriter discovers there's a problem and issues a decline. In this instance, it was exceedingly alarming because the rejection came after the family had moved into the home. It is pretty frightening to have your family counting on you, and you are helpless, at the mercy of an underwriter, and wondering what to do if you all end up homeless.

LESSONS LEARNED

It is not only a mortgage professional's reputation that matters, but also what he or she can do for you. The loan officer may be referred by Realtors and be highly regarded, but if that professional doesn't specialize in serving physicians, he or she can run clients into a bad place.

A loan officer who specializes or deals with physicians regularly can get loans approved for FHA, and sometimes even conventional financing that other lenders/underwriters will decline. This type of loan officer will understand how to take a client whose student loans are showing a zero payment and walk that client through the process of getting enrolled in IBR and then qualifying for a loan based on the lower IBR amount, which is what we ended up doing in Dr. Schwartz's case.

WHY THE ENDS MATTER MORE THAN THE MEANS

It is not which type of loan you end up with, but how you get there. Interestingly, we were able to get Dr. Schwartz approved for an FHA loan. He had some delinquent student loans that dropped his scores. He had come out of med school temporarily because of a medical issue in the family. When he did that, his student loans came out of deferral. He had reapplied, but the application either was not received or not approved. It was about this time that he moved. This happens all the time when student loan notifications cross paths with people who move and don't have a new mailing address. Because of this, he could not meet the minimum credit score requirements for the physician home loan product that we use for residents, and he couldn't qualify for a conventional loan for multiple reasons.

The other lender had also been trying to get Dr. Schwartz approved for an FHA loan but was not able to find a solution. We found a solution using a two-pronged approach. We calculated what his monthly payment would be on an IBR and we got the underwriter to allow us to use the lower IBR amount to qualify. We also added his father as a cosigner on the loan. Between those two creative methods of dealing with the problems at hand, we were able to get him approved. Here's the key reason why. We were only able to think through that solution and all the moving pieces because we had helped many physicians and seen many complicated situations in the past. In Dr. Schwartz's case, it was not that we had the magic loan program; it was that we had the magic loan team: the loan originator, processor, and underwriter all got on the same page and were able to identify and execute a solution strategy that addressed the numerous issues under a very stressful and short timeline.

CHAPTER 5

HOME LOAN OPTIONS FOR THE RESIDENT OR FELLOW GOING INTO PRACTICE

The challenges the new attending physician is going to face are similar to those of the resident physician. The main difference between them might be that the higher income among attending physicians allows for more flexibility.

CASE 2

TYPICAL CHALLENGES NEW ATTENDING PHYSICIANS FACE

Chris is a typical physician moving from residency to attending, with high-700 FICO scores, $25,000 to $50,000 in cash/reserves, relatively low consumer debt, and student loans of $200,000.

Chris signed a two-year, noncontingent employment contract with Ronald Reagan UCLA Medical Center for $200,000 per year.

Three challenges Chris and newly attending physicians commonly face are:

- He has a less than 20 percent down payment.

- His employment contract start date is July 1 and he would like to close on June 1 to have time to move his family into the home.

- His student loan deferment period is ending and his loan repayment is to begin soon, but as of yet, payment amounts do not show up on his credit report.

CHRIS'S OPTIONS ARE:

FHA or VA Home Loan

- **Down payment.** Not required with VA. FHA will allow it to be gifted, and requires no liquid assets or reserves in addition to the 3.5 percent down. Chris would have enough for a down payment with FHA or VA.

- **Closing.** Closing 30 days before employment with a multiyear, noncontingent contract is allowed by *some* underwriters for VA and FHA loans, but most will want to see at least one pay stub prior to closing. This is a potential problem. Chris will want to make sure underwriting has approved his employment start date before he makes an offer, commits to a closing date, and packs the U-Haul for California.

- **Student loans.** Student loans in deferment or forbearance 12-plus months from the closing date are not counted into the debt-to-income ratio for VA or FHA. However, student loans that do enter into repayment within 12 months would be factored into underwriting debt-to-income ratios. In Chris's case, as is the case with most deferred student loans, the $200,000 student loans report a balance but with no payment on the credit report. When no payment amount has been determined or is reported, underwriting guidelines call for 2 percent of the outstanding balance to be used against Chris's debt-to-income ratio. Therefore, an FHA underwriter will have to count at least $4,000 as the monthly payment, which should still work for Chris, based on the income amount specified in his contract.

The downside to an FHA loan is that it has a significant mortgage insurance premium, which, with higher-value homes, can really add up. FHA currently charges 1.75 percent as an up-front mortgage insurance premium, in addition to the 1.35 percent annual fee (paid monthly) for the life of the loan. This can be a real detractor for FHA financing.

Conventional Home Loan

- **Down payment.** Chris should qualify with as little as a 5 percent down payment on loan amounts up to $417,000, and as little as 10 percent down on high-balance loans up to $625,500 (this depends on the county where you buy and can change from year to year), as long as he's using his own seasoned funds and he can document those funds with at least one full monthly bank statement.

- **Closing.** Closing 30 days before the start of employment is possible with a multiyear, noncontingent contract, but Chris will find that most banks and underwriters are not comfortable with taking future income into consideration and will require at least one, if not two, pay stubs before allowing him to close. This is a gray area in the conventional guidelines, left up to the underwriter's discretion, but most conventional lenders don't deal with physician contracts

WHY PHYSICIAN HOME LOANS FAIL

regularly and are not comfortable allowing borrowers to close with just a contract and no pay stubs.

- **Student loans.** Student loans in deferment and showing no monthly payment amounts on credit still must be counted against the debt-to-income ratio. In Chris's case, even though he hasn't started to repay his student loans, conventional underwriting will calculate student loan payments between $4,000 and $10,000 (2 percent and 5 percent of balance) per month against him. With his starting salary of $16,666 per month, he might still qualify. However, if he's looking to purchase a house in a high-cost area, this could present a challenge. Most conventional guidelines will cap Chris at a 45 percent debt-to-income ratio, or total outgoing expenses of $7,500 per month. If he has $4,000 going to pay student loans, he is left with about $3,500 for home and any other consumer debt payments, provided he can find an underwriter who uses the 2 percent payment calculation and not the 5 percent, which varies from bank to bank.

This is another example of conventional underwriting's rigid guidelines that can make it tough for physicians to qualify, due to high student loan balances. Three to six months down the road, Chris's credit report would likely be updated with actual payments, usually much less than 2 percent to 5 percent of the outstanding balance. At that time, conventional financing would be much easier to obtain, but if Chris needs to buy today, a conventional loan could be a challenge for him. Again, going through the credit and income approval process early, before house hunting has begun, would be advised. A good loan officer, specializing in serving physicians, should be able to guide Chris through this and offer several solutions.

Physician Home Loan

- **Down payment.** This really varies depending on the region where the home is being bought. Most physician home loans require 5 to 10 percent down, depending on the price of the home. However, a few banks are still making 100 percent physician loans, mostly at lower loan amounts, and most are located on or near the East Coast. There are currently several banks offering physician home loans in high-cost areas such as California. They offer loan amounts up to $1.5 million with as little as a 5 percent down payment. We've tried to list as many of these lending solutions as possible at www.USPhysicianHomeLoans.com.

- **Closing.** Closing 30 to 60 days before employment is possible with sufficient liquidity, or post-closing reserves, which usually means having funds to cover three to six months (depending on the bank and its specific underwriting requirements) of the monthly mortgage payment. For example, if Chris were to put 5 percent down ($20,000) on a $400,000 home, and he had $8,000 in closing costs for a total of $28,000 cash out of pocket, then, in addition to that $28,000, underwriting would want to see that he had an additional $9,000 to $18,000 (the equivalent of three to six monthly mortgage payments of $3,000 each) in savings somewhere.

- Reserves are required by most banks because they anticipate that borrowers are going to spend money on relocating, they're going to spend money on movers and getting settled, and they want to see that borrowers have some savings. This will make underwriters comfortable that you can make your first couple of mortgage payments before you bank any money from your employment contract.

- **Student loans.** A physician home loan does *not* usually count student loans that are not currently in repayment. However, in the case of payments coming due in the near future, underwriting may calculate a monthly payment around 1 percent of the outstanding balance. This would not disqualify Chris at his attending income level.

The challenges of purchasing a home with the minimum down payment, the ability to close on future income from an employment contract, and having significant student loans in deferment or forbearance are pretty much nonissues with the physician home loan. One, if not all, of those challenges is likely to be an issue with FHA, VA, and conventional loans. With a physician home loan, Chris would avoid mortgage insurance, likely have a much better home-buying experience, and be able to close and move into his new home prior to starting his new position.

A TRUE STORY: DR. GILBERTSON

Dr. Gilbertson had two unique challenges. As he talked to numerous conventional lenders before making his way to us, he found that his down payment was not sufficient and that a closing date before starting employment was impossible with those he had spoken to. He was stepping into his first attending position, with a substantial income of about $260,000 a year. The trouble was that he had not yet received a dime of that salary, making closing funds tight. He only had sufficient funds for about a 5 percent down payment. He and his wife had already found and commenced construction on a beautiful, brand-new home for around $425,000. He could easily afford that on his new salary, but his low down payment limited his loan options, because a conventional loan requires more money down to avoid costly monthly mortgage insurance.

The initial lenders Dr. Gilbertson spoke to also would not allow him to close on a conventional loan until he had two full paycheck stubs. Because of his start date and how the payroll worked at his hospital, he would have to have been on the job for about 40 days before he received his second paycheck stub. This meant that Dr. Gilbertson would, essentially, have had to move himself, his three children, and his spouse into temporary housing, which is tough to find for a family of five, and work for 40 to 50 days before closing on the new home. That didn't appeal to him or to his wife.

When Dr. Gilbertson came to us, we were able to find a physician home loan product for him that included a low 5 percent down payment, required no mortgage insurance, and allowed a closing date that was a full 30 days before he started his employment contract. He was able to relocate, move in, get situated, and start his employment thereafter.

Dr. Gilbertson's story is commonplace among our newly attending physician clients. The biggest issues typically being little money for a down payment and the need to close before the new position start date.

The physician home loan products are geared to accommodate these situations, offering a common-sense approach to home financing that conventional and other traditional loans lack.

LESSONS LEARNED

- **Before making an offer, know when you can close.**
  Being able to close before starting his position was a huge

benefit for Dr. Gilbertson and his family. It prevented them from having to move twice, and allowed them to get settled before Dr. Gilbertson started his new position. This is a very important point to clarify with your loan officer. I'd also suggest you specifically ask the underwriter to give you the earliest date the closing could take place, to make doubly certain you are on the same page and there are no surprises.

- **Higher cost up front can equal more savings later.** Although the closing costs and interest rate of a physician home loan product with less than 20 percent down can be higher than a traditional loan with the same percentage down, we were able to compensate for that by avoiding mortgage insurance. This saved Dr. Gilbertson thousands of dollars over the lifetime of his loan.

CHAPTER 6

HOME LOAN OPTIONS FOR SELF-EMPLOYED AND 1099 CONTRACTOR PHYSICIANS

In addition to the challenges already described (down payment, student loans, and closing prior to employment start date), physicians transitioning to self-employed or 1099 independent contractor status have the challenge of proving to an underwriter what their income will be. Before I present a case scenario, I'll clarify the different view that underwriters have of W-2 noncontingent contract borrowers (hourly or salary) self-employed, and 1099 independent contractor borrowers.

HOW UNDERWRITING VIEWS SELF-EMPLOYED AND 1099 CONTRACTOR BORROWERS

Income for self-employed and 1099 contractors is not cut and dried. Employment contracts for independent contractors are usually based on the number of patients treated, or on a percentage of collections. Sometimes, a contract specifies a dollar amount per hour but not necessarily a guaranteed number of hours. This is not helpful for the underwriters and does not give them a definitive means of arriving at monthly income. Even if the practice you're contracting with has more work than it can handle and you're told that you can work as much as you want—virtually endless work available—there's no guarantee that you will decide to work that many hours because, by definition, if you are a 1099 independent contractor, the employer can't require you to show up and leave at specific times. According to the IRS code, what defines independent contracting is that it's not an employee–employer relationship in which the number of hours (and, therefore, income) is mandated. When the borrower has no history of independent contracting or of self-employment, underwriters have no proof of a quantifiable and consistent income they can sign their name to.

HOW SELF-EMPLOYED AND 1099 CONTRACTOR PHYSICIANS CAN VERIFY INCOME

With a physician home loan, there is definitely an ability to close before you have a two-year employment history, but your ability to get financing will still vary based on how much information your lender can obtain about your future income. How much information they receive depends on the type of work situation you are in and how willing the practice is to put guarantees into writing.

CASE 3

INCOME VERIFICATION FOR 1099 CONTRACTOR PHYSICIANS

Here, the two income types are portrayed as two different physician clients. Dr. Smith is taking a 1099 contractor position and Dr. Jones is self-employed.

Dr. Smith could represent a variety of 1099 contractor working situations, including:

- An emergency medicine physician who has signed a contract that spells out the number of hours and rate of pay;

- An anesthesiologist who joined an anesthesiology group that serves multiple local hospitals and will be paid a percentage of the collections that the group bills each hospital;

- A dentist who may work at two or three different dental offices and will be paid either a percentage of the collections or a fixed daily rate.

The hospital or practice where Dr. Smith is going to work can provide one of two verifications of income:

- A contract that reads, "Dr. Smith will be available to work a minimum of 40 hours per week and she will be paid this rate. Of course, she can work more, but she will make herself available to work at least 40 hours."

- A letter that reads, "Here's what other 1099 contractor physicians in our practice make. Here's the range and the average salary. Every physician is guaranteed at least 40 hours a week of work, or will work X number of days per week at a specific daily rate."

Both of these examples are obviously paraphrased contract examples but provide a strong indication for what the 1099 contractor physician's income is going to be.

If the hospital or practice does not provide clear indications of income, most often in the form of an employment contract or

WHY PHYSICIAN HOME LOANS FAIL

offer letter, as well as plain English projections of income, then Dr. Smith will probably have to work for six months before qualifying for a physician home loan, and two years before qualifying for a conventional home loan. This happens when the hospital or practice says it will pay a percentage of the collections or a percentage of the profitability, or when the letter is loosely written with no discernible guarantee of income. In such a situation, even physician home loan underwriters will likely ask for a six-month work history and advise trying again, once the doctor has some history on the job.

The take-away here is that 1099 positions present additional challenges for financing. You will not know if you will qualify for sure until you go down the road of speaking with a physician mortgage specialist, gathering whatever documentation you can from your employer, and presenting it to an underwriter for approval. My advice is to avoid being too gung-ho, making offers and falling in love with homes, until you have crossed the bridge of getting your financing fully credit and income approved by an underwriter.

INCOME VERIFICATION FOR SELF-EMPLOYED PHYSICIANS

Dr. Jones could be buying an existing medical practice, starting his own practice, or becoming a partner in a practice. In all instances, he is considered self-employed. In this situation, an underwriter will not be able to quantify Dr. Jones's future income, because it's totally wide open. How do you quantify what the expenses will be? How do you quantify what the gross and net income will be once he takes over the business? In the end, it's likely the underwriters won't be able to arrive at an income figure they are comfortable with until Dr. Jones has been in practice for at least six months before qualifying for a physician home loan, and several years for a conventional loan. How long he has to wait depends on how those numbers look six to

12 months down the road and how the situation is presented to an underwriter at that time.

Underwriters, both physician and conventional, are looking for consistent income that can be reasonably expected to continue. When they can quantify that kind of income, they are comfortable signing off on the loan and putting their name on it. When income is nebulous, financing is going to be nearly impossible with any lender anywhere, and a track record of at least six to 12 months is very likely to be required.

DOCTOR JONES AND DOCTOR SMITH HAVE THE FOLLOWING OPTIONS:

Conventional, FHA, or VA Home Loan

- **Self-employed and 1099 contractors.** Whether the physician is self-employed or a 1099 independent contractor, the traditional conventional financing guidelines will require a two-year history of income, which must be verified by the two most recent years' tax returns. The underwriter will arrive at a monthly income amount by averaging the past two years' returns. This can be a long run for both physicians. For instance, if Dr. Jones is just starting his self-employment in July 2014, the partial year in 2014 likely won't show much income, maybe four or five months' worth. We also frequently see losses in the first year's tax returns, due to the gap between the new patients' first visit and the doctor's receipt of the payment, the purchase of new equipment, and other first-year expenses. In all likelihood, he'll have to work all of 2015 and 2016 before he has two full years of profitable tax returns to qualify for a conventional mortgage. There are exceptions to this. For example, if he showed sufficient income between part of 2014 and the full year of 2015, it would be possible to get a conventional underwriter to approve the loan in early 2016, once the 2014 and 2015 taxes were done, but this still means he'd have a minimum of two years to wait before buying a new house via conventional, FHA, or VA financing. As a side note, with higher down payments, it is sometimes possible to get a conventional approval with just one year's business tax returns rather than two. This is becoming less and less likely, as Fannie and Freddie continue to tighten their automated underwriting engines and seem to be headed toward requiring two years of self-employed returns.

Physician Home Loan

- **The 1099 independent contractor.** If Dr. Smith can provide a contract and/or a letter from the practice or hospital clearly articulating a guaranteed hourly/daily rate and number of hours/days available, or if she is going from W-2 to 1099 status and is basically just changing employers, it's possible for her to obtain financing before she starts her new position. This is pushing the guidelines to the extreme, but with a 10 to 20 percent down payment, she should be able to find an underwriter who will allow it.

- **Self-employed.** If Dr. Jones is truly going into private practice on his own, most physician programs will require that he be on the job for a minimum of six months. Most underwriters will want to see business bank statements, a profit-and-loss for the practice, any background information on the practice (such as past years' returns), and documentation that the practice is thriving and growing since he started there.

Although it will depend on your location and which bank you choose and what its particular guidelines are, the physician home loan product will allow you to close sooner and finance larger loan amounts, with less money down, and without mortgage insurance.

A TRUE STORY: DR. FINKEL

Dr. Finkel, a dentist, purchased the dental practice that he frequented as a child in his hometown. When he bought the practice, it had been running for about 25 years, and much of the equipment looked as old. He began updating the equipment immediately. The retiring dentist was, as Dr. Finkel referred to him, an "old-school dentist" who hadn't kept up on the newest techniques and didn't have the latest technology and equipment.

Dr. Finkel worked alongside the retiring dentist for six months before buying the practice, and subsequently ran it on his own for six months before coming to us for a loan on his first home. Within that first 12-month period, he had massively increased collections by almost 35 percent. His net cash flow was about $30,000 a month, which is very impressive for a dentist who has only been out of dental school for one year.

Dr. Finkel's practice was thriving. He was accumulating savings and paying down the new dental equipment and technology upgrade loans way ahead of schedule. He had a sound business plan and had bought a great practice. It seemed everything was going his way. He and his wife began looking for homes overlooking the town where he had grown up and where he had returned to raise his family. They thought it would be easy to qualify because he had excellent credit, savings for a down payment, and had made a significant amount of money in the last six months.

They found a modest but beautiful home more quickly than they had expected. It was near the golf course and within the boundaries of the church he had attended in his youth. After viewing the home and meeting with their Realtor, they decided to make an offer. The offer was accepted and they were overjoyed. Finally, their vision of their future family would be complete. The next step was to secure financing. They had 40 days to be out of their rental and into their new home. Naturally, the Realtor who had helped his parents buy their last home and was *the* area expert and knew a loan officer, whom he had worked with for years and years. The referred loan officer was certain he could get the loan processed and closed within their agreed-upon settlement deadline.

Fortunately, the loan officer was indeed very good. Dr. Finkel and his wife met with him, and within 30 minutes he had told them it was impossible to get financing without at least one more year's self-employment tax returns. He suggested the only option available was to have their parents buy the home as rental property and sell it back to them the next year, when they could qualify. Dr. Finkel was not about to ask the parents for any more help. He and his wife were determined to stand on their own.

As I recall, Dr. Finkel had been to five different lenders, including the bank where he did his personal and business banking, the credit union where his wife had banked since she was 18 years old, and several other loan officers and mortgage brokers their Realtor had referred them to. They all came to the same conclusion: they needed two years of tax returns, but they should at least come back and give it a try once the upcoming year's returns were filed. It looked as if Dr. Finkel was six to 18 months away from being financed for a new home.

To her credit, Dr. Finkel's wife was very persistent. She just wouldn't give up on her new home. They'd started their family when they we're both in college and they had lived on a shoestring budget through dental school and training. They now had four children and had outgrown their rental, and she was determined not to extend the lease for another year. She did some research online before searching for "physician loans Utah" and finding us. When she called, I asked the usual questions: How long have has your husband been in practice? What did he do prior to that? How long was the practice in existence? After I got the whole backstory, I told her that I thought it was a stretch but possible, and I'd take on the challenge if she were willing to help me put together what I needed to correctly frame it to underwriting. At first, she laughed. She was so used to hearing "No." I had to reassure her that we had a chance and I believed we could help her.

As we reviewed Dr. Finkel's financials, we were able to create a picture of consistent income, which was likely to continue: The dental practice had been in existence for 25 years and the past two years' income was very solid. With Dr. Finkel's arrival in the practice, the numbers continued to improve. The six most recent bank statements from the practice showed a steady increase in gross collections each month, which matched the profit and loss and also showed increasing net income.

We documented the file with a complete history of the practice, the previous two years' practice returns, and every shred of financial evidence we could find to show the practice was booming. We asked the underwriter to allow us to use the practice profit from the previous two years under the former owner, even though our client's income was skyrocketing higher. Our client's income was 30 to 50 percent higher per month than the practice's average monthly income for the previous two years. The underwriter carefully reviewed the income documentation and agreed the whole picture made sense. She signed off on the loan. Boom! Six months into the practice, we put Dr. Finkel and his family in a house. It was beautiful.

LESSONS LEARNED

You need a mortgage professional who can make a good case for you. Dr. Finkel needed a mortgage professional who could persuade an underwriter by painting a picture of consistent income likely to continue. We were able to do this by providing the following documents:

- The practice's tax returns for two years before Dr. Finkel bought it;

- Profit and loss statements for the practice's previous 12 months, which comprised the six months when Dr. Finkel was in training with the previous dentist, and the six months after he took over the practice;

- Business bank statements for the six months after Dr. Finkel bought the practice.

We showed that the practice's income for the previous two years had been very consistent. The first month Dr. Finkel started in the practice, the income began to creep up. Within one month of his taking over the practice, collections started to surge. This was because he began servicing more patients and he was able to provide more services with the new dental equipment he had brought into the practice. A couple of years later, Dr. Finkel's practice was thriving and he bought a second practice. He and his wife were recently able to refinance their home loan with us because the rates had gone down and they had seen a significant increase in their home's equity. It was awesome to see them doing so well and a privilege to have been able to help them.

You need an underwriter who has the ability to judge risk. Hypothetically, if you compare the security of Dr. Finkel's income going forward with that of someone working at J. C. Penney who has a salary of $50,000 a year, sure, that salary is easier to quantify and easier to underwrite in a standardized process. However, certainly from a risk perspective, if I were investing in that mortgage, I would put my money on Dr. Finkel's ability to continue paying the mortgage as agreed.

If J. C. Penney were to close down tomorrow, the employee making $50,000 a year would be in trouble. Someone with a career in retail likely has a lot less chance of making money than Dr. Finkel has going forward. Not only does it make sense to invest in Dr. Finkel's loan when he is starting out in his career, but it's also a safer loan, in my opinion. However, it's harder to underwrite because it requires an underwriter who is good at judging risk. Conventional underwriters don't have the latitude to judge risk. That's not their job. Their job is to follow the rigid underwriting guidelines they are given to the letter of the law. Is the loan application a square peg that fits a square hole? The underwriters' primary job is to make sure the application fits conventional loan underwriting guidelines, whereas physician underwriters conduct more risk analysis and make decisions based on some common sense.

A physician home loan is likely most advantageous for young, self-employed, and 1099 physicians, due to the underwriters' greater latitude in analyzing risk, a luxury not afforded to the conventional, FHA, or VA underwriter.

CHAPTER 7

WHAT TO EXPECT AT THE CLOSING

A lot goes into your closing day. You can count on no less than a dozen people working on your home loan the day of signing and recording the loan into your name. It's a complex last stage, with a lot of moving pieces, and missing something can cause delays. If you're working with the right professionals, you should expect your closing to go very smoothly. You should have good communication from the loan originator, or from his or her team, leading up to your closing. You should have a good idea of the cash needed for closing and have wire instructions on where to send your funds before the closing date. Unfortunately, I've heard plenty of horror stories ranging from closing delays and misunderstandings about the amount of cash due at closing, to the nasty surprise of finding that the underwriter had declined the loan application at the last minute. Here are a few things you can do to protect yourself.

HOW TO PREPARE FOR THE CLOSING

As soon as you've written an offer on a house and it has been accepted, you should begin to think about the closing day. Make certain to send a copy of the purchase agreement to your lender within 24 hours. I suggest you send it personally, as soon as you are able, to ensure there is no miscommunication between your Realtor and loan officer. Within three days of your loan officer receiving a copy of the purchase agreement between you and the seller, you will receive a written good-faith estimate (GFE). This is a guarantee of fees, loan program, and rate lock verification based on the home you have agreed to purchase. Make sure you carefully review the GFE with your lender, either on the phone or in person. As mentioned before, the current GFE leaves out vital information (such as the amount of the final payment with taxes, insurance, and HOA) and the projection of the amount of cash needed to close, including all closing costs and prepaid items (such as home-owner-association transfer fees, prorated interest, taxes and insurance based on your specific settlement date and the property you are buying).

I recommend being very specific with your loan officer. Ask for a written, estimated settlement statement or closing worksheet, something that shows the total amounts of cash needed to close and the down payment. Let your loan officer know you are looking for a written projection of all final numbers, one that is as accurate as humanly possible at this point.

IMPORTANT COMMUNICATION BETWEEN YOUR LENDER AND YOU

From the day your purchase agreement is accepted to the closing day, it is important to alert your lender of any changes to your financial situation that might affect your loan, or other changes that could prevent the transaction from going smoothly.

You should receive weekly updates from your lender, which will let you know where you are in the process and that everything is on track. If you are not receiving a weekly communication, I would recommend a weekly call or e-mail with the loan officer, to ensure

WHAT TO EXPECT AT THE CLOSING

everything is going smoothly and you are on schedule for the closing date. It's always a good idea just to confirm with your loan officer that the settlement will take place prior to the expiration of your interest rate lock. This is particularly important if there have been any delays that have set back the closing date.

Confirm the date of your closing, how you should transfer funds to the title company, and where you're physically going to be on that date. You should receive wire instructions and a pretty good estimate as to what your cash-to-close figure is going to be, if that has changed at all from the beginning of the transaction. Your loan officer and Realtor should organize all of this in the week leading up to the closing.

SETTLEMENT STATEMENT REVIEW

Somewhere between 24 hours and 48 hours before the closing, you should have a copy of what's called the HUD-1 Settlement Statement. This is a standardized form created by the U.S. Department of Housing and Urban Development (HUD), which is used across the country, coast to coast. It is the final settlement statement, which explains where all the money is coming from and to whom those funds are going. It contains the purchase price of the home, your new loan amount, the amount of your deposits or earnest money, any seller-paid closing costs, prepaid taxes, and insurance and/or assessments that need to be paid to the homeowner's association or municipalities.

YOUR CASH TO CLOSE

Once you total all those debits and credits, the bottom line is your cash to close, the final dollar amount you need to bring to consummate the transaction. You should have the cash-to-close figure and a HUD-1 Settlement Statement in hand prior to your arrival at the title, escrow, or settlement company. I'd recommend you ask your loan officer to make sure this happens, as it gives you an opportunity to review everything, make sure the fees are correct, and all the terms are as you expected, and allows for time to send your wire before you arrive at the title or escrow company to sign.

TIMING OF THE CLOSING

In an ideal situation, you'll receive the final settlement statement 24 to 48 hours beforehand. There are a few things that might prevent this from happening:

- **If you're on a short closing deadline**. Generally, anything less than 30 days from the day your offer is accepted to the closing is considered a short closing deadline.

- **If some turmoil or delays during underwriting affected the process**. This could happen, for instance, if your down payment funds were not verifiable in your accounts or there was some kind of appraisal or inspection problem or delay. Under these circumstances, you may not have that final settlement statement until the day of closing.

SIGNS OF TROUBLE: WHEN TO ASK QUESTIONS

If your loan officer is not ramping up communication a week before closing, it's time to start asking questions. The reality is that sometimes things come up—emergencies, funerals—and your loan officer may be off his or her A-game. Know that a week out from closing, you'd be wise to start asking to be updated. Don't be afraid to ask your loan officer to confirm that everything is on track and there is no sign of delay or trouble.

CLOSING REMOTELY BEFORE YOU ARRIVE AT YOUR NEW HOME

The way a remote closing is handled may vary across the country, depending on whether you're in a title or escrow state and whether it's customary to use attorneys or an escrow or title company for signing. Generally speaking, there are three things about a remote closing that you need to keep in mind:

- Where will you physically be on the settlement date?

- Will you be able to sign and return all the documents in time for the settlement deadline in your purchase agreement?

- How are you going to transfer your down payment?

Where Will You Physically Be on the Settlement Date?

If you're nearing your settlement date and you're not going to be within miles of your new home, you need to bring that up to your Realtor and loan officer. It's a good idea to communicate with both. You can send a simple e-mail that says, "Hey, as a reminder, we're within a week of closing and I'm not going to be in Nevada." Just put it on their radar. If you're working with good professionals, they will be used to organizing transactions remotely. However, just to be safe, make sure that it's not overlooked. A miscommunication can add several days to the transaction.

Can All Documents Be Signed and Returned in Time?

The closing documents go from the lender's office to the title, escrow, or attorney's office, where the final settlement statements are prepared and a package is printed and ready for the closing the following day.

Most of these packages are in excess of 100 pages, and they all need to be signed, initialed, or notarized. This is not something that you want to do via e-mail, because there's too much that can be overlooked. For an in-town closing, hypothetically scheduled on Friday, the 30th, your loan officer can send the documents to the title office on the 28th or 29th. For a remote closing, a good loan officer will know that he'll need to send the documents on the 26th or the 27th at the latest if the settlement deadline is on the 30th.

Let's say I was financing a home for you in Nevada and I thought you'd be in Nevada on the closing date, which is Friday, the 30th. I've told the team that we need to have closing documents out to the title company in Nevada on the 29th so that, on the 30th, you can come in and sign on the settlement deadline. Then I find out on the 29th that you're not going to be in Nevada on the 30th. You're going to be in Colorado. The title company will have to ship the package overnight to Colorado, which means you'll receive it on the 30th. Although you may be signing the documents on the 30th and may be able to transfer your money on the 30th, the home will still not be yours until the deed has been recorded at the county recorder, where your new home is located. Even if you overnight them to Nevada, they will still arrive on the 31st, the day after your closing. You've missed your settlement deadline. If there is a delay, you could lose your interest rate, or even the property itself, by defaulting on the closing deadline. Bottom line: make sure to communicate your whereabouts to your Realtor and loan officer before the closing.

How Are You Going to Transfer Your Down Payment?

Buyers who are relocating often overlook having a plan for how to move money. Let's say you're moving from Alabama to Nevada, and around the time of closing you could be in Alabama or somewhere

WHAT TO EXPECT AT THE CLOSING

else, such as in Colorado, visiting your parents. Wherever you are when you get that final cash-to-close number, you will have to know how to wire money. Can you wire electronically? Can you wire by phone? About a week before the closing day, you really need to think through how you'll move your money. It's not that you must wire money a week earlier than closing day, but you want to be in communication with your bank about your plans. Explain to your bank that you're going to be in Colorado, but you are currently in Alabama. The wire needs to get to Nevada. How do you set that all up?

It will behoove you to make these arrangements before you leave Alabama or the state where you're banking. That is key. If you don't, you could have a problem. For example, if you bank with Bank of America and are moving to Utah, then you'll need to know that Bank of America has no branches in Utah. None. If, on closing day, you don't have a wire agreement set up with Bank of America, you'll have to drive to a state that has a Bank of America branch, sign a wire agreement, order your wire, and then drive back to Utah!

FAQS ABOUT YOUR HOME LOAN CLOSING

Will There Be Any Surprises the Day I Close My Physician Home Loan?

This is a common question. If you found the right lender up front and have been doing your part since, there should not be any surprises on the day of closing. That means you have been supplying all of the necessary information in a timely fashion, communicating your whereabouts and expectations, and making yourself accessible to everyone involved.

As stated earlier, it would be wise to get an update on what your payment and cash-to-close projection will be. E-mail your loan officer the financing proposal or the last closing projection document that you received and ask if anything substantial or significant has changed. Is this amount about what I can still expect? Have there been any changes to the tax, insurance, or interest rate? Is everyone still on the same page? When you're contacting your loan officer, be sure to remind him or her where you will be on the day of closing.

If there is a "surprise" at closing, it is often the result of a miscommunication on the part of the originator, the borrower, or both. This can be avoided if you make sure that you, the Realtor, and the loan officer are all in agreement on the way that your closing will be conducted.

How Do I Ensure a Successful Closing?

When I hear this question, my mind goes back to the beginning of the decision-making process. The way you ensure a successful closing is to pick the right loan officer up front. If this person is a knowledgeable, skilled specialist who has navigated dozens or hundreds of successful physician transactions in the past, they are likely going to be able to do it again.

As discussed earlier, finding the right mortgage professional means asking yourself the following questions: Are you working with someone who is experienced with relocating physicians? Are you working with someone who has testimonials from a resident physician, newly attending, or self-employed physician? Have you spoken to one of your originator's previous clients or read their testimonials? Is there a good amount of evidence that this person is a full-time, fully knowledgeable professional, with many years in the business and many happy clients? If you can answer yes to all these questions, then 98 percent of the time your due diligence will pay off and you can expect to have a happy closing.

―――― CHAPTER 8 ――――

COMMON MISTAKES WHEN BUYING A HOME

FAILING TO INSIST ON A FULL CREDIT AND INCOME APPROVAL

A preapproval issued by a loan officer is simply not enough in today's post-mortgage-meltdown world. Typically a preapproval entails only a quick application and a credit report. The way mortgages used to be underwritten was simply, "You've got your $50,000 for down payment and I'm looking at your paycheck stub, I can use your base salary, and we're done." That's not going to bring to light anything out of the ordinary in a tax return or an employment contract, or anything out of the ordinary about where your down payment is coming from. It's just a snapshot overview.

A quick preapproval will also not consider whether your spouse has a side business and whether there are losses in that side business. Let's say that you're a physician buying a home in California. Your wife or your husband has a side business with significant losses, and California is a community property state. Those losses could count against your debt-to-income ratio. Not accounting for the losses early in the loan process could result in a declined loan later, when you have a house on the line.

I recommend providing all documents to the underwriters up front. By insisting on a very detailed and pre-underwritten credit and income approval, you can insulate yourself from the majority of issues and dreaded surprises. We don't want that final underwriter saying, "Whoops! Your down payment money is not acceptable," because he noticed a $20,000 deposit on a bank statement that wasn't submitted earlier in the process. We want to have already gone through that hurdle and cleared it with our original pre-underwriting application.

Remember that even with a full credit and income approval, your file will be seen by an underwriter at three different points during the transaction and unforseen problems can certainly come up anytime throughout the transaction. "Oh, the appraisal didn't come in. There's a title issue." There's always a chance there could be some additional conditions that you need to clear up before the loan receives its final underwritten approval and clear to close. If you've wisely chosen your loan officer and completed a full credit and income approval, they'll probably be minor, but clients should not assume that everything's going to be peaches and cream. It's a much more stringent underwriting environment today, and it's paramount that you make it all the way through the credit and income approval process as early as possible to flush out any foreseeable glitches early in the process.

DECIDING ON A LENDER PURELY BASED ON COST

Closing costs and interest rates are important and should be considered in your decision, but you also have to consider what type of service you will be experiencing throughout the process. You may

COMMON MISTAKES WHEN BUYING A HOME

save a few dollars in closing costs by going with a discount lender, but in doing so, you may have also added more hours of work to get through underwriting, had sleepless nights, and spent money to keep your family in a hotel for a week because they missed your closing deadline.

I'm going to preach on this one, because more often than not, when I speak to physicians who have been surprised by a last-minute, declined loan application, it's because they selected their lender based solely on the lowest rate and cost. They failed to ask for referrals, testimonials, or anything that substantiated the lender as an expert in his or her field. This can be the kiss of death. The least expensive loan officer is oftentimes the one with the least amount of experience and expertise.

It's important to recognize whether your loan is a slam dunk that anyone can handle with their eyes closed, or if it has some additional complexity, such as relocation, closing with a contract before you have pay stubs, student loans going in or out of deferment, IBR, jumbo loan amount, or complicated employment situations.

This is not all that different from the medical world. The more highly skilled and specialized you are, the higher your fee is likely to be. Although the skill of a mortgage professional does not compare to that of a highly skilled surgeon, the principle holds true. The least skilled offer discounts and pander for business; the most highly skilled have plenty of referral business and are not likely to do the job for 50 percent off. Truth be known, a lender can't hire top-quality professional staff and give significant discounts to every client. It's a clear-cut choice between the A team and the B or C team. You have to decide whom you want to trust with your new home loan.

If you were to shop for a lender purely based on rate and cost, you'd find lenders who compete by doing lots of volume and offering a discounted fee. The main problem with a volume-based business is that these lenders will typically not be able to give the same level of expertise, attention, and service to a more complex transaction.

MISSING PURCHASE CONTRACT DEADLINES

This mistake is more often the fault of the loan officer or Realtor who fails to emphasize the importance of contractual dates or neglects to provide important information about a contractual date. Most of our clients, especially those who are relocating, have a tremendous amount going on. They may be studying for board certifications or taking final exams, on top of getting their kids and family ready to relocate and move across the country. These added stresses could make it difficult to keep focused on all of the contractual deadlines involved in a home purchase. There are so many important dates to remember: inspection, financing approval, home appraisal, when to wire funds, settlement closing/funding, and delivery of keys. The timing of things must be perfect, because your earnest money and your home are on the line. Everyone must know and understand the important dates, and communication between Realtor, loan officer, and client must be seamless.

Here is an example of why it pays to work with someone who knows the nuances and is experienced working with relocating physicians. In some states, you receive the keys to your home on the day of closing or settlement. Basically, you receive the keys the day you sign. In Utah, "settlement" means the date when you sign your documents. The transaction isn't recorded or finalized until the next business day. If your settlement date is on a Friday and you're planning to arrive in Utah Friday morning and move in Friday afternoon or Saturday

COMMON MISTAKES WHEN BUYING A HOME

morning, that's a real problem, because you're not actually going to take title to the property until Monday.

Both the Realtor and the loan officer should be advising you on what exactly occurs on the contractual settlement date. They should ask you when you plan to move into the home. If you're on a tight schedule and plan on arriving in Utah on Friday and moving in on Saturday, then your closing actually needs to take place on Thursday. In a remote closing, you would need to sign the documents on Wednesday and overnight them back to Utah so they arrive on Thursday and your transaction can be recorded Friday and you can get the keys that day. A delay of only a day can make a huge difference when everything you own is packed and you are counting on a home where you can unload it.

A TRUE STORY: DR. FISH

Dr. Fish, a surgeon, was coming out of fellowship. He was recruited by a practice across the country that was a subgroup of a larger hospital network. His employment contract was complicated, although not that uncommon, in that he had one contract with the large hospital network and another contract with the subgroup he was actually going to be working with on a day-to-day basis. All in all, the contract was about 50 pages long and very detailed. What Dr. Fish did not realize was that his income status was that of a 1099 independent contractor, a fact that was about to throw a wrench into things.

While house hunting, he decided to have a new house built. He contacted a home builder, signed a contract, and they began construction. As is typical with new construction, the builder recommended his preferred lender. Unfortunately, the preferred lender

WHY PHYSICIAN HOME LOANS FAIL

was not specialized or experienced in working with physicians and took the easy approach to preapproving Dr. Fish. The loan officer pulled his credit, wrote him a preapproval letter, and sent him on his way to write a $12,000 nonrefundable deposit, select upgrades, and commence construction.

Dr. Fish told the loan officer that he had a base salary of $25,000 a month, as well as incentives above and beyond that: ranging from $10,000 to $20,000 a month. The loan officer for the builder qualified him on this verbal information and moved forward. Dr. Fish logically concluded financing would not be a problem. He was a highly sought-after surgeon with perfect credit and did not think twice about moving forward.

His common-sense analysis was correct. There is no doubt he was capable of debt servicing the loan amount he was after, but unfortunately, he did not understand, and the loan officer failed to explain, the extremely rigid guidelines of conventional mortgages regarding income.

The home was two weeks away from being completed and the movers were scheduled. Dr. Fish and his family had planned to relocate across the country in two weeks, to arrive at their new home a few days before he was to start his new employment. He received a call from the builder's loan officer, who informed him that after the loan had made it to underwriting, the underwriters had reviewed his employment contract and discovered Dr. Fish was to be a 1099 independent contractor, which, unfortunately, would require a two-year history of income before they could qualify him for the loan. He was declined and likely out $12,000 in nonrefundable earnest money.

When Dr. Fish contacted me, he told me he could not believe he was having a problem getting financing. He was going to be making a tremendous amount of money. His payment was only $3,000 a month. How in the world could he possibly not get approved for financing? Fortunately, we were able to qualify him for our physician home loan program and it all worked out beautifully in the end, closing within just a couple of days of his original close date.

LESSONS LEARNED

Don't Be the Hare!

In Aesop's fable *The Tortoise and the Hare*, the hare loses the race because of his overconfidence. To a certain degree, physicians can feel overly confident in their ability to qualify for a loan. That exacerbates the problem, especially if they're working with a loan officer who is not familiar with working with doctors and their unique financing challenges. The average loan officer won't know how to advise them and convince them that they need to gather all of those documents up front. When a physician resists providing those documents, experienced physician loan officers have to say, "Absolutely, it's necessary. Here's why." We have to work hard to bring about greater understanding on why it's truly important we move through that the credit and income approval step as early as possible in the process.

Beware of "Preferred" Lenders.

The word "preferred" can be misleading. In a sense, it means the person doing the recommending has worked with the lender before and knows the lender is successful with typical buyers. "Preferred" sounds good, but it's not necessarily good if the preferred lender doesn't have experience serving physicians and have access to physician home loans. In some cases, builders will require or incentivize you to go through their preferred lender. So how do you get around that? How would you get the underwriter's full credit and income approval? The answer is that you must insist on it.

First, you should be aware of any of the factors that we've identified as adding complexity to the transaction (student loans, new employment, relocation, down payment not sitting in your account for several months leading up to the purchase, and self-employed or independent contractor status), which could cause a conventional underwriter to decline your loan. Clearly tell the preferred loan officer, "This is not a vanilla loan. There could be some complications here."

Second, tell the preferred loan officer that you'd like him or her to do more than just the preapproval. You would like to request a full credit and income approval from an underwriter.

A very similar situation can happen when talking to a Realtor before finding a loan officer. Let's say you and your spouse come into town to meet with a Realtor, who takes you to look at a house. You walk into the house and it's perfect. You weren't sure whether you were going to buy or rent, but this one is in your price range, it's by the hospital, and it's in the best school district. It's perfect!

When you've found the perfect home but haven't worked through the process of financing, nine times out of ten you're going to work with whatever financing person the Realtor recommends, because you are out of time and the Realtor's loan officer is the only one who is going to pick up the phone at 6 p.m. on a Saturday. The Realtor is going to assure you that his referral is a professional with a good track history. It will sound something like this, "If you want this home, you need to work with someone we know who can move quickly through this process. It's Saturday. We'll get them on the phone right now."

It happens all the time. Everyone is in a hurry. The "preferred" or recommended loan officer does a really quick preapproval and moves on. It's not until the file hits the underwriter's desk that the loan officer realizes there's a problem.

CHAPTER 9

KEY POINTS FOR PHYSICIANS

OVERVIEW OF THE LIFE OF A LOAN

When mistakes or upsets occur, it's often because clients don't fully understand the complexity of the loan process. I believe fully understanding the process will help lead you to a smooth transaction. Here, I provide a quick overview of the life of a loan.

Pre-underwriting

The first part of the loan process is probably the most important part. It's important that you understand the difference between a preapproval, which is an extremely cursory review of your loan application and credit, and a full credit and income approval. A credit and income approval analyzes not only your credit and student loan situation to quantify all those payments and calculate the debt-to-income ratio correctly, but also your current and future income (pending and new employment contracts), if the down payment source is allowable, as well as consideration of the closing date in relation to your new employment start date.

Truly, an underwriter has underwritten everything pertaining to you as a borrower. At that point, all you have left to do is just go through the appraisal, title work, and, of course, write your purchase agreement.

Home Appraisal

Once you have written an offer and the seller has accepted it, we order your appraisal. We pull the title report on the property and make sure there are no unknown liens or encumbrances. Once we have processed all the appraisal, title, and property information, we're going to repackage the loan so that it can be submitted to your final underwriter in perfect condition.

Final Underwriter Approval

The final underwriter is the gatekeeper, the last person who can approve the loan and essentially release the money for the mortgage. The loan goes back through the underwriting process and will receive what's called a "conditional approval." This means that the loan is approved, typically, with a few conditions. Those conditions could be additional comparables for an appraiser, or more details of an employment contract, or something on the credit report that needs additional clarification. There always seem to be a few conditions that need to be fine tuned before the closing. The loan and the final conditions then go back into underwriting again for the final "clear to close." Once that's received, closing documents go out.

The loan process is much more detailed and labor intensive than it was before the mortgage meltdown. When you receive your approval with additional conditions, you should not feel it is out of the ordinary or that you're being scrutinized more than everyone else is. It is just part of the process in today's mortgage environment.

A TRUE STORY: DR. PETERS'S PERFECT TRANSACTION

Before I review the six steps to a flawless home purchase, here is another true story. Unlike the stories you've read thus far, this story is of a physician client of ours who orchestrated the perfect transaction. He could not have done it any better. Without coaching, just from intuition, and with a little extra due diligence, he orchestrated a flawless home purchase.

Dr. Peters built a conservative home in a great neighborhood when he started his practice. His home had been built in a brand-new subdivision, which was now about six or seven years old and had fully matured. The house directly across the street from him was one of the last homes to be built in the subdivision, and it was his wife's dream home from the minute it was framed. It was what they wished they could have built when they built their home. It was bigger, had nicer finishes, a beautiful pool in the backyard, and was near their church and in their children's school district. It was truly perfect.

Over the previous six or seven years since starting in practice, Dr. Peters had paid off most of his student loans. He now had more income and fewer expenses. Lo and behold, their neighbors, the owners of the house across the street, mentioned they were going to sell their home. The timing was perfect and Dr. Peters's wife was ecstatic about finally getting her dream home.

Dr. Peters started researching lenders. He called a few doctor friends but found that none of them had particularly enjoyed working with the loan officers they had selected, and he was unable to get a good referral. He went online, searching for "physician home loans," and found our site. He called me and we had a nice 30-minute conversation discussing his situation. He had some unique factors. He had made a few bad investments and although he had paid off all of his debt, he hadn't accumulated the savings that he wished he had for a down payment. A physician home loan looked as if it would work well for him, because he needed a loan amount over the jumbo limits and he had less than 20 percent to put down.

After our conversation, Dr. Peters continued his due diligence. He went to our website and read all the testimonials. As it turned out, he knew two of the clients with whom we'd worked. One was a doctor and the other was a member of Utah Medical Association Financial Services, and also Dr. Peters's financial planner. He called them both to ask them about their experience with us.

When we had our second phone conversation, Dr. Peters was certain he was comfortable moving forward with us. We had a great relationship and great trust, because he really had done his due diligence and research up front. I told him that before he wrote his offer, he should allow me to gather all of his documents and get him a written credit and income approval, which he could present with his offer. We were not in a huge hurry and we didn't have to write an offer immediately.

Dr. Peters was very prompt in getting me all the documents I needed. We submitted his file for initial credit and income approval, and the file came back the next day, underwriter approved. He then was able to make a very strong offer to his neighbor.

When he presented his offer, he was able to attach a copy of the underwriter-signed credit and income approval, which was basically the equivalent of a cash offer. No Realtors were involved and he said he would close in two weeks. Needless to say, the seller loved the strength of the offer and agreed to give my client a bit of a discount, as this was going to be much easier than he had thought.

LESSON LEARNED

"There are more things in heaven and earth, Horatio, than are dreamt of in your philosophy."

—WILLIAM SHAKESPEARE, *HAMLET*

The most important takeaway is that there is more to know in the world of physician mortgages than anyone who is not a full-time specialist in physician loans could possibly know. The single best thing you can do is work with an expert, ideally someone who has access to physician mortgage products and has an extensive history of happy physician clients. You can find a list of such physician lenders at USPhysicianHomeLoans.com, which provides a guide to lenders who specialize in physician home loans.

SIX STEPS TO A FLAWLESS HOME PURCHASE

1. Choose a Mortgage Professional Who Can Educate and Truly Guide You

If you just do one thing, ensure you start off on in the right direction by locating a mortgage professional who has experience with physicians and has done a good job with physician clients in the past.

If you spend extra time and energy to find the right person and then allow that professional to guide you through the process, you're much more likely to get to closing without a hitch. Physicians often run into trouble when they think that there is no reason that they shouldn't get financing. For instance, the resident who was able to get a home loan back in 2006, before the mortgage meltdown, and who is now making significantly more money may think that getting a home loan today should be easy and one that any bank would finance. However, the physician may not be taking into consideration all of the factors, such as being a 1099 independent contractor, or closing on the new home prior to starting the new position. Both of these factors would throw a huge wrench into things for a conventional mortgage lender.

The reality is that a lot has changed and under the lens of the post-mortgage-meltdown underwriting guidelines, getting a loan is not as easy as it used to be. If there's a deficiency or complexity in your situation, you need an expert to guide you through the loan process and all possible solutions. Nobody is better able to do this than someone who specializes in physician home loans. That person has seen all the same challenges before and has an arsenal of outside-the-box solutions.

2. Verify Your Lender's Reputation

Once you think you've identified a good loan officer, verify his or her reputation. Look for past client testimonials and don't be afraid to ask how many doctors they have worked with in the past few months. If you don't get a good vibe or you're not sure, I'd advise you to keep looking or ask to speak with a few of their past physician clients.

Once you've identified several loan officers in your area who appear to be experts, who have testimonials, and who look as if they serve physicians on a regular basis, the next step is to have a good phone conversation with them. Take a few minutes to cut out all distractions. Don't call from the freeway or emergency room (I've literally had a call from an anesthesiologist in the middle of a procedure). Find a place and time you can focus on the mortgage professional you are interviewing. Let that person know about any challenges you can see, such as student loans, relocation to a new state and/or job, your source of down payment, and ask a couple of intelligent questions. You will know in your gut whether the mortgage professional is the real deal.

3. Obtain a Credit and Income Approval

A preapproval is simply not enough for you to gamble your family's new home on. I advise you insist upon a full credit and income approval. I cannot emphasize enough the importance of getting all credit and income documents into the hands of an underwriter as early in the process as possible.

The thing to keep in mind is that the underwriter is the one who has the final say. Finding a seasoned loan officer who is experienced with doctors is a great first step, but at the end of the day, it doesn't matter how good your loan officer thinks your file is, because he or she is not the final decision maker. It's not like a mom–dad situation where the underwriter and loan officer meet in the middle. It's like a parent–child situation, and the parent in this situation is the underwriter. That's where the buck stops. Get all of your income, new employment contracts, student loan changes, and down payment documents all the way to the underwriter and insist on a full credit and income approval. Once you have that, you're ready to rock.

If you follow these first three steps of the six steps to a flawless home purchase, you should be in great shape. The only way you could be more prepared to buy a home is if you had the money in the bank and were prepared to write a check for the entire purchase price. But there are a few more things you can do to ensure the rest of your transaction is flawless.

4. Carefully Select Your Realtor

Your Realtor should, preferably, not be just someone who's qualified in helping the average person move across town. You are looking for someone with relocation experience, ideally physician relocation. You should be able to find such Realtors through an online search, via referral from the medical department you are joining, a colleague who has recently relocated to the area, or a referral from a loan officer specializing in physician home loans. If you can't find a Realtor with experience in physician relocation, then the next best thing is a Realtor who specializes in relocation, because that person will have more specialized knowledge of the potential pitfalls and be attuned to serving clients remotely.

Remember, the timing of your employment contract start date, relocation, and remote closing all add complexity to the transaction. The Realtor who is the biggest short-sale or foreclosure specialist in the county might be capable of doing amazing things for his or her short-sale clients. She or he may be busy and sell more homes than anyone else. However, that same busy Realtor, if not experienced in the nuances of relocation, is more likely to forget the remote closing timeline and leave you keyless on move-in day. I see it much more frequently than anyone would like.

A great Realtor will plan the transaction with you, pull out a sheet of paper, talk through all the dates with you, and literally map out the transaction. That way, when he or she is structuring the offer and the deadlines, everything flows and matches, so you don't get to the end of the deadline, and realize your family is homeless for two weeks because of a delay on the seller's side or because the Realtor and loan officer were not in communication about when your loan could close.

5. Stay in Communication

Make sure everyone has the same dates in mind for the loan approval, wiring of closing funds, loan document signing, and move-in date. This is especially important for relocating physicians, who often have movers scheduled and a relatively short timeline to move in and get settled before starting their new position. Make it a point early in the transaction, even before you write up your offer or go house hunting, to get your loan officer and Realtor on the same page. It is important that these two

KEY POINTS FOR PHYSICIANS

advisors are in communication about loan type, financing, and appraisal deadlines, as well as the all-important closing and move-in date.

What can happen in the transaction is that everybody gets focused one thing, such as the appraisal, or the outstanding final signed employment contract, and they take their eye off the relocation part of the transaction and end up missing a date.

If you get into the habit of staying in communication with your Realtor and loan officer throughout the transaction, you'll prevent a lot of problems. It is as easy as firing off an e-mail to both parties saying, "Hey, team, I'm selling my house on Wednesday and I'll be in Ohio that day. I need to move in and have keys Friday afternoon for the Arizona home. Everybody on board, do you see any problems with those dates?"; "Hey, did you get everything you need from me? Is there anything else you need?"; "My financing appraisal deadline is coming up this Friday. Just wanted to make sure that was on everybody's radar and we were not going to have any problems with that."; "Hey, team, just verifying that the financing and appraisal deadline is next Monday, which means my earnest money is nonrefundable. Can you confirm we are good to pass this date?"; or, "Hey, team, closing deadline is a week away. I'm confirming that everything is set and my family will be in a moving van on Wednesday." For anything having to do with deadlines or the dates when you will be traveling, I would recommend being in direct communication with both the Realtor and the loan officer.

The frequency of your communication may vary depending on the transaction, but I think once or twice a week is probably the recommended dosage. That's not too much and not too little. If you send communications a couple times a day or daily, you're going to drive everybody crazy.

Even if you are working with a great Realtor and loan officer team, keep in mind that things happen. The loan processor goes on vacation, the kids get sick, real-life stuff happens, and things can slip through the cracks. As a consumer, if you're not communicating what your expectations are with the deadlines, you're leaving yourself open to possible mistakes.

6. Be Proactive

Take responsibility for the deadlines you sign on your purchase agreement and ensure you don't lose your earnest money. This is truly your responsibility as the buyer, and all you have to do is to be aware of your inspection, appraisal, financing, and settlement deadlines. I find most homebuyers rarely know that deadlines in a purchase agreement even exist. It's extremely seldom that we get any kind of communication from the client following up on these dates. Typically, this is because their Realtor rushed through the purchase agreement and did not bring it to the client's attention.

But at the end of the day, this is on you. You are the one who is risking your earnest money. You can do this simply by paying attention to the dates in your purchase agreement and set yourself reminders to follow up with your real estate and mortgage team before the dates are upon you and your money is lost.

Follow this advice and you have a 99 percent chance that your transaction will be a flawless and enjoyable one!

———————— *APPENDIX A* ————————

Good Faith Estimate (GFE)

OMB Approval No. 2502-0265

Name of Originator	Citywide Home Loans, A Utah Corporation	Borrower	
Originator Address	4001 South 700 East #250 Salt Lake City, UT 84107	Property Address	TBD
Originator Phone Number	801-747-0200		
Originator Email		Date of GFE	08/02/2013

Purpose — This GFE gives you an estimate of your settlement charges and loan terms if you are approved for this loan. For more information, see HUD's Special Information Booklet on settlement charges, your Truth-in-Lending Disclosures, and other consumer information at www.hud.gov/respa. If you decide you would like to proceed with this loan, contact us.

Shopping for your loan — Only you can shop for the best loan for you. Compare this GFE with other loan offers, so you can find the best loan. Use the shopping chart on page 3 to compare all the offers you receive.

Important dates
1. The interest rate for this GFE is available through 08/02/2013 05:00 PM . After this time, the interest rate, some of your loan Origination Charges, and the monthly payment shown below can change until you lock your interest rate.
2. This estimate for all other settlement charges is available through 08/16/2013 05:00 PM .
3. After you lock your interest rate, you must go to settlement within NA days (your rate lock period) to receive the locked interest rate.
4. You must lock the interest rate at least 10 days before settlement.

Summary of your loan

Your initial loan amount is	$ 540,000.00
Your loan term is	30 years
Your initial interest rate is	4.500 %
Your initial monthly amount owed for principal, interest, and any mortgage insurance is	$ 2,736.10 per month
Can your interest rate rise?	☑ No ☐ Yes, it can rise to a maximum of %. The first change will be in
Even if you make payments on time, can your loan balance rise?	☑ No ☐ Yes, it can rise to a maximum of $
Even if you make payments on time, can your monthly amount owed for principal, interest, and any mortgage insurance rise?	☑ No ☐ Yes, the first increase can be in and the monthly amount owed can rise to $. The maximum it can ever rise to is $
Does your loan have a prepayment penalty?	☑ No ☐ Yes, your maximum prepayment penalty is $
Does your loan have a balloon payment?	☑ No ☐ Yes, you have a balloon payment of $ due in years.

Escrow account information — Some lenders require an escrow account to hold funds for paying property taxes or other property-related charges in addition to your monthly amount owed of $ 2,736.10 .
Do we require you to have an escrow account for your loan?
☐ No, you do not have an escrow account. You must pay these charges directly when due.
☑ Yes, you have an escrow account. It may or may not cover all of these charges. Ask us.

Summary of your settlement charges

A	Your Adjusted Origination Charges (See page 2.)	$ 6,695.00
B	Your Charges for All Other Settlement Services (See page 2.)	$ 8,657.63
A + **B**	Total Estimated Settlement Charges	$ 15,352.63

Calyx Form - GFE2010_1.frm (12/09), Rev. (9/10)

Good Faith Estimate (HUD-GFE) 1

WHY PHYSICIAN HOME LOANS FAIL

Understanding your estimated settlement charges

Your Adjusted Origination Charges

1. Our origination charge This charge is for getting this loan for you.	6,695.00
2. Your credit or charge (points) for the specific interest rate chosen ☐ The credit or charge for the interest rate of [ ] % is included in "Our origination charge." (See item 1 above.) ☑ You receive a credit of $ **0.00** for this interest rate of **4,500** %. This credit **reduces** your settlement charges. ☐ You pay a charge of $ [ ] for this interest rate of [ ] %. This charge (points) **increases** your total settlement charges. The tradeoff table on page 3 shows that you can change your total settlement charges by choosing a different interest rate for this loan.	0.00
A **Your Adjusted Origination Charges**	$ 6,695.00

Your Charges for All Other Settlement Services

Some of these charges can change at settlement. See the top of page 3 for more information.

3. Required services that we select These charges are for services we require to complete your settlement. We will choose the providers of these services. **Service** **Charge** **Appraisal** 475.00 **Credit Report** 34.00	509.00
4. Title services and lender's title insurance This charge includes the services of a title or settlement agent, for example, and title insurance to protect the lender, if required.	1,940.00
5. Owner's title insurance You may purchase an owner's title insurance policy to protect your interest in the property.	2,500.00
6. Required services that you can shop for These charges are for other services that are required to complete your settlement. We can identify providers of these services or you can shop for them yourself. Our estimates for providing these services are below. **Service** **Charge** **Service** **Charge**	
7. Government recording charges These charges are for state and local fees to record your loan and title documents.	85.00
8. Transfer taxes These charges are for state and local fees on mortgages and home sales.	
9. Initial deposit for your escrow account This charge is held in an escrow account to pay future recurring charges on your property and includes ☒ all property taxes, ☒ all insurance, and ☐ other [ ]	1,725.00
10. Daily interest charges This charge is for the daily interest on your loan from the day of your settlement until the first day of the next month or the first day of your normal mortgage payment cycle. This amount is $ **66.5753** per day for **15** days (if your settlement is [ ]).	998.63
11. Homeowner's insurance This charge is for the insurance you must buy for the property to protect from a loss, such as fire. **Policy** **Charge** **Hazard Insurance** 900.00	900.00
B **Your Charges for All Other Settlement Services**	$ 8,657.63
A + **B** **Total Estimated Settlement Charges**	$ 15,352.63

Good Faith Estimate (HUD-GFE) 2

Calyx Form - GFE2010_2.frm (12/09), Rev (9/10)

APPENDIX A

Instructions

Understanding which charges can change at settlement

This GFE estimates your settlement charges. At your settlement, you will receive a HUD-1, a form that lists your actual costs. Compare the charges on the HUD-1 with the charges on this GFE. Charges can change if you select your own provider and do not use the companies we identify. (See below for details.)

These charges cannot increase at settlement:	The total of these charges can increase up to 10% at settlement:	These charges can change at settlement:
• Our origination charge • Your credit or charge (points) for the specific interest rate chosen (after you lock in your interest rate) • Your adjusted origination charges (after you lock in your interest rate) • Transfer taxes	• Required services that we select • Title services and lender's title insurance (if we select them or you use companies we identify) • Owner's title insurance (if you use companies we identify) • Required services that you can shop for (if you use companies we identify) • Government recording charges	• Required services that you can shop for (if you do not use companies we identify) • Title services and lender's title insurance (if you do not use companies we identify) • Owner's title insurance (if you do not use companies we identify) • Initial deposit for your escrow account • Daily interest charges • Homeowner's insurance

Using the tradeoff table

In this GFE, we offered you this loan with a particular interest rate and estimated settlement charges. However:
• If you want to choose this same loan with **lower settlement charges**, then you will have a **higher interest rate**.
• If you want to choose this same loan with a **lower interest rate**, then you will have **higher settlement charges**.

If you would like to choose an available option, you must ask us for a new GFE.

Loan originators have the option to complete this table. Please ask for additional information if the table is not completed.

	The loan in this GFE	The same loan with lower settlement charges	The same loan with a lower interest rate
Your initial loan amount	$ 540,000.00	$	$
Your initial interest rate [1]	4.500 %	%	%
Your initial monthly amount owed	$ 2,736.10	$	$
Change in the monthly amount owed from this GFE	No change	You will pay $ more every month	You will pay $ less every month
Change in the amount you will pay at settlement with this interest rate	No change	Your settlement charges will be **reduced** by $	Your settlement charges will **increase** by $
How much your total estimated settlement charges will be	$ 15,352.63	$	$

[1] For an adjustable rate loan, the comparisons above are for the initial interest rate before adjustments are made.

Using the shopping chart

Use this chart to compare GFEs from different loan originators. Fill in the information by using a different column for each GFE you receive. By comparing loan offers, you can shop for the best loan.

	This loan	Loan 2	Loan 3	Loan 4
Loan originator name	Citywide Home Loans			
Initial loan amount	$ 540,000.00			
Loan term	30 years			
Initial interest rate	4.500 %			
Initial monthly amount owed	$ 2,736.10			
Rate lock period	NA days			
Can interest rate rise?	NO			
Can loan balance rise?	NO			
Can monthly amount owed rise?	NO			
Prepayment penalty?	NO			
Balloon payment?	NO			
Total Estimated Settlement Charges	$ 15,352.63			

If your loan is sold in the future

Some lenders may sell your loan after settlement. Any fees lenders receive in the future cannot change the loan you receive or the charges you paid at settlement.

Calyx Form - GFE2010_3.frm (12/09), Rev. (9/10)

 Good Faith Estimate (HUD-GFE) 3

127

WHY PHYSICIAN HOME LOANS FAIL

Citywide Home Loans, NMLS# 67180

TRUTH-IN-LENDING DISCLOSURE STATEMENT
(THIS IS NEITHER A CONTRACT NOR A COMMITMENT TO LEND)

Applicants:
Property Address: **TBD**

Application No:

Prepared By: **Citywide Home Loans, A Utah Corporation**
4001 South 700 East #250
Salt Lake City , UT 84107
Date Prepared: **08/02/2013**   Ph: **801-747-0200**

ANNUAL PERCENTAGE RATE	FINANCE CHARGE	AMOUNT FINANCED	TOTAL OF PAYMENTS
The cost of your credit as a yearly rate	The dollar amount the credit will cost you	The amount of credit provided to you or on your behalf	The amount you will have paid after making all payments as scheduled
* 4.527 %	$ * 447,690.12	$ * 537,306.37	$ * 984,996.49

☐ REQUIRED DEPOSIT: The annual percentage rate does not take into account your required deposit

There is no guarantee that you will be able to refinance to lower your rate and payments

INTEREST RATE AND PAYMENT SUMMARY

	Rate & Monthly Payment
Interest Rate	4.500 %
Principal + Interest Payment	$ 2,736.10
Est. Taxes + Insurance (Escrow)	$ 575.00
Total Est. Monthly Payment	**$ 3,311.10**

☐ DEMAND FEATURE: This obligation has a demand feature.

☐ VARIABLE RATE FEATURE: This loan contains a variable rate feature. A variable rate disclosure has been provided earlier.

SECURITY: You are giving a security interest in: **TBD**

☑ The goods or property being purchased   ☐ Real property you already own.

FILING FEES: $ **85.00**

LATE CHARGE: If a payment is more than **15** days late, you will be charged **5.000** % of the payment.

PREPAYMENT: If you pay off early, you ☐ may ☑ will not   have to pay a penalty.
                                         ☐ may ☑ will not   be entitled to a refund of part of the finance charge.

Page 1 of 2

Calyx Form - NEWTIL1.frm (11/12)

APPENDIX A

Citywide Home Loans, NMLS# 67180

Application No:	Date Prepared: **08/02/2013**

CREDIT LIFE/CREDIT DISABILITY:

Credit life insurance and credit disability insurance are not required to obtain credit, and will not be provided unless you sign and agree to pay the additional cost.

Type	Premium	Signature	
Credit Life		I want credit life insurance.	Signature:
Credit Disability		I want credit disability insurance.	Signature:
Credit Life and Disability		I want credit life and disability insurance.	Signature:

INSURANCE:

The following insurance is required to obtain credit:

- ☐ Credit life insurance
- ☑ Property insurance
- ☐ Credit disability
- ☐ Flood insurance

You may obtain the insurance from anyone you want that is acceptable to creditor.

☐ If you purchase ☑ property ☐ flood insurance from creditor you will pay $ for a one year term.

ASSUMPTION:

Someone buying your property
☐ may
☐ may, subject to conditions
☑ may not assume the remainder of your loan on the original terms.

See your contract documents for any additional information about nonpayment, default, any required repayment in full before the scheduled date and prepayment refunds and penalties.

☑ * means an estimate
☑ all dates and numerical disclosures except the late payment disclosures are estimates.

You are not required to complete this agreement merely because you have received these disclosures or signed a loan application.

THE UNDERSIGNED ACKNOWLEDGES RECEIVING A COMPLETED COPY OF THIS DISCLOSURE.

Applicant	Date	Applicant	Date
Applicant	Date	Applicant	Date
Prepared By	Date		

Calyx Form - NEWTIL2.frm (11/12)

APPENDIX B

Citywide Home Loans, NMLS# 67180

FEES WORKSHEET
Fee Details and Summary

Applicants:		Application No:	
Prepared By:	Citywide Home Loans, A Utah Corporation Ph. 801-747-0200	Date Prepared:	08/02/2013
	4001 South 700 East #250, Salt Lake City, UT 84107	Loan Program:	30 YR FIXED

THIS IS NOT A GOOD FAITH ESTIMATE (GFE). This "Fees Worksheet" is provided for informational purposes ONLY, to assist you in determining an estimate of cash that may be required to close and an estimate of your proposed monthly mortgage payment. Actual charges may be more or less, and your transaction may not involve a fee for every item listed.

Total Loan Amount: **$ 540,000**   Interest Rate: **4.500 %**   Term/Due In: **360 / 360 mths**

Fee	Paid To	Paid By (Fee Split**)		Amount	PFC / F / POC
ORIGINATION CHARGES					
Loan Origination Fee		Borrower	1.000%	$ 5,400.00	✓
Processing Fee		Borrower		$ 500.00	✓
Underwriting Fee		Borrower		$ 795.00	✓
OTHER CHARGES					
Appraisal Fee		Borrower		$ 475.00	
Credit Report Fee		Borrower		$ 34.00	
Closing/Escrow Fee	TITLE COMPANY	Borrower		$ 350.00	✓
Document Preparation Fee	TITLE COMPANY	Borrower		$ 50.00	✓
Lender's Title Insurance	TITLE COMPANY	Borrower		$ 1,485.00	
Endorsements	TITLE COMPANY	Borrower		$ 55.00	
Owner's Title Insurance	TITLE COMPANY	Borrower		$ 2,500.00	
Mortgage Recording Charge	TITLE COMPANY	Borrower		$ 85.00	
Hazard Insurance Reserves		Borrower	$ 75.00 x 3 mth(s)	$ 225.00	
County Property Tax Reserves		Borrower	$ 500.00 x 3 mth(s)	$ 1,500.00	
Daily Interest Charges		Borrower	$ 66.5753 x 15 day(s)	$ 998.63	✓
Hazard Insurance Premium		Borrower	$ 75.00 x 12 mth(s)	$ 900.00	

TOTAL ESTIMATED FUNDS NEEDED TO CLOSE:				TOTAL ESTIMATED MONTHLY PAYMENT:	
Purchase Price (+)	600,000.00	Loan Amount (-)	540,000.00	Principal & Interest	2,736.10
Alterations (+)		CC Paid by Seller (-)	5,000.00	Other Financing (P & I)	
Land (+)		Lender Credit	0.00	Hazard Insurance	75.00
Refi (incl. debts to be paid off) (+)		Seller's Credit Owner's Policy	2,500.00	Real Estate Taxes	500.00
Est. Prepaid Items/Reserves (+)	3,623.63	Cash Deposit on sales contract	5,000.00	Mortgage Insurance	
Est. Closing Costs (+)	11,729.00			Homeowner Assn. Dues	
				Other	
Total Estimated Funds needed to close			62,852.63	**Total Monthly Payment**	3,311.10

* PFC = Prepaid Finance Charge   F = FHA Allowable Closing Cost   POC = Paid Outside of Closing
** B = Borrower   S = Seller   Br = Broker   L = Lender   TP = Third Party   C = Correspondent

Calyx Form - feews.frm (09/2010)

CPSIA information can be obtained
at www.ICGtesting.com
Printed in the USA
BVOW03s0148091216
470285BV00001B/1/P